# THE
# EMBRACE
# METHOD

How to leverage your trauma and pain
to live the life of your dreams!

# THE
# EMBRACE
# METHOD

How to leverage your trauma and pain
to live the life of your dreams!

**VLADIMIR LOUISSAINT**

# THE EMBRACE METHOD

*How to leverage your trauma and pain to live the life of your dreams!*

# DEDICATION

*To my son, Fidel, a.k.a Lito, and my beloved wife, Julie, you both are the brightest lights in my life.*
*The joy and acceptance you both bring to me, are what my wildest dreams are made of. For eternity and beyond, and every fiber of my being, I love you both.*

# TABLE OF CONTENTS

# INTRODUCTION

T here I was, sitting in my work-assigned cruiser as it was parked in our three-car garage, valiantly fighting back the tears that were gushing out of my face. "C'mon man, just put your best game face on and go inside. Jules shouldn't have to deal with this" I tearfully said to myself. How was I supposed to walk into our home and convince my wife that everything was fine as if only a mere few days ago, I did not almost end my life? I had barely come to terms with it myself, nothing made sense, and unlike almost every other crisis I've ever faced, I couldn't laugh, perform, or bury this one away.

As I walked inside, and put the very firearm that could have been crime scene evidence away in our safe,

and stepped into our bedroom where my wife was working from home, she smiled at me and said, "How was your day bunny?" I lost all control and crumbled into her arms. This moment, albeit immensely painful, was a defining moment for me; one that would end the shame that had been secretly eating away at my very soul.

Now, how could a guy who's always presented as so cheerful, positive and funny be struggling so deeply in secret? That day marked the beginning of my journey of putting myself back together, and what I would later discover with a childhood rife with complex trauma, attachment issues, undiagnosed ADHD, and fragile self-esteem, is that somewhere along the way I lost my true self and thus, an inability to embrace who I was. If you're reading these words today, chances are that someone you know or you have stories similar to this one. In fact, the World Health Organization estimates that approximately 380 million people worldwide suffer from depression, and those people are more likely to have developed depression as a result of an adverse childhood experience. Often, without

intervention, we are unable to find an identity outside of what has happened to us, and move throughout our lives reliving those experiences and emotions, without ever healing and growing from them.

Through sharing my own life experiences and journey of self-discovery, I will explain how embracing and understanding our pain can transform the way we see the world and ourselves, and change the trajectory of our lives. Those who read this book will learn how to face their past, harness the transformative power of forgiveness and healing, and live the life of their dreams by acknowledging and accepting themselves.

I struggled in childhood and throughout my adult life with low self-esteem, brought on by chaos and trauma at home. Throughout my life I had adopted a superficial identity that was pleasing and unassuming to the world, as well as the practice of burying my unresolved issues as deeply as I could, which resulted in greater mental health challenges that nearly ruined my life.

Thank God I was inspired to help my readers understand that they are never alone in their own quest, and that a world of possibilities for their lives is embedded within them.

This book is presenting a thorough method by which one will dig deep into the depths of their past, be encouraged to reflect and engage with themselves, and embrace the very essence of who they truly are.

What this book is not, however, is a replacement or substitute for therapy or counseling with a licensed professional. What readers learn in this book will be an important undertaking that can supplement other mental health interventions or treatment. As a reminder, if you or someone you know is struggling with a mental health crisis or thoughts of self-harm, please reach out to someone you trust for help, call 988, or text HOME to 741741. Remember, help is always there as long as you're willing to have it.

Let's get ready to EMBRACE!

EMBRACING YOUR PAIN IS THE FIRST STEP TOWARD TRANSFORMING IT INTO POWER.

# CHAPTER 1

# ACKNOWLEDGING YOUR PAST - EMBRACING YOUR STORY

Have you ever felt the weight of the past pressing down on your shoulders? Maybe there's that memory you've tried so hard to bury, an incident you wish never occurred, or a choice you deeply regret. Or, perhaps, there's a trauma that's left an indelible mark on your psyche. Many people carry these burdens, and some even feel it's something they should hide, something they wish had never happened. It's crucial, though, to realize that acknowledging your past is the first step towards a brighter future. It's the foundation upon which you can build the life you've always dreamt of.

You see, in my community and possibly in yours, the dominant message has often been about just "living". The idea is simple: life happens, and you move on. There's no space for processing, understanding, or truly feeling the weight of our experiences. My own journey was punctuated with voices that echoed a similar sentiment. Whenever I felt the sting of rejection from my absentee father or any other wound from the past, my mother would often tell me, "Don't waste your tears. Just move on." This approach, while seemingly practical, not only pushes the pain aside but also shrouds our genuine emotions in shame.

In embracing our stories and acknowledging our pasts, it's crucial to understand the essence of feeling our feelings honestly. It's about truly experiencing and accepting your unique truth, not a narrative crafted to fit someone else's mold. The weight that many carry, be it the loss of a parent, the chaos of their households, or dealing with the challenges of a differently-abled sibling, is often met with the overarching command of execution. "Just do. Don't feel. Feelings don't pay bills. Feelings don't change the past," they say.

And yet, when we look deeper, when we scratch beneath the surface of risky behaviors, self-harm, and behavioral addictions, we find a myriad of unacknowledged feelings and traumas. These suppressed feelings and buried traumas manifest in ways that are often destructive. Take, for instance, the young boy who arrives drunk at a youth program. What drives a 12-year-old to such extremes? There's something deep, something unacknowledged and buried, pushing him to the brink.

The mindset many enter life with is rooted in suppression: "I'm not supposed to talk about this. None of this even matters." And when these suppressed feelings find an outlet, they often come out as anger, a defense mechanism against the world's perceived judgments. So, when you read this, when you start this journey of acknowledging your past, understand that it's about genuine self-reflection. It's about feeling those buried feelings and understanding that they have shaped you. But, more importantly, it's about using that understanding to reshape your future. As you move forward through these chapters, my hope is that you see yourself reflected, and you find the strength to say, "This is me. This is my story. And it's okay."

Life is, in many ways, a tapestry woven from our experiences, emotions, and interactions. Yet, many of us are conditioned early on to suppress certain threads of this tapestry, keeping them hidden from the world and, often, from ourselves. These suppressed threads are usually the ones tinted with pain, embarrassment, or any emotion we've been taught to perceive as 'negative.' Over time, this suppression becomes second nature. But like a dam holding back water, when the pressure becomes too much, it bursts forth, often manifesting as anger, a powerful emotion that serves as armor against the world's perceived judgments. However, this eruption isn't just about releasing suppressed feelings. At its core, it's a plea—a plea for understanding, a plea for acceptance, and most importantly, a plea to be seen and heard.

From a young age, many are conditioned to believe that vulnerability equates to weakness. Expressions like "Big boys don't cry" or "It's not that big of a deal" form a mental barrier. This barrier convinces us that our feelings are invalid or that expressing them will make us burdensome to others. This suppression isn't always explicit. Sometimes, it's the unsaid words, the subtle societal nudges, or the fear of judgment that mutes our inner voice. But these emotions, when suppressed, don't just vanish. They simmer beneath the surface, waiting for a release. And in moments of pressure or triggering events, they can explode in ways that might seem disproportionate to the immediate cause. This eruption is less about the trigger and more about the pent-up feelings seeking an outlet.

To navigate the maze of suppressed emotions, it's essential first to recognize and validate them. This journey begins with self-reflection. Genuine self-reflection is about granting yourself permission to delve into those hidden corners of your psyche. It's about acknowledging that while some memories might be painful or embarrassing, they're integral parts of who you are.

Engage in introspective practices. These can range from meditation and journaling to art and therapy. These

platforms create a safe space for you to confront, understand, and eventually come to terms with your feelings.
Through this process, you'll likely uncover patterns or triggers that lead to suppression. Recognizing these can help
you navigate them better in the future. Unpacking suppressed feelings isn't just about understanding the past; it's
about leveraging that understanding to shape a brighter,
more genuine future. By acknowledging the role suppressed emotions have played in your past actions or
reactions, you gain the power to respond differently in the
future. More so, by embracing your complete emotional
tapestry, you start viewing yourself holistically. This acceptance allows you to step into spaces with authenticity
and confidence. It grants you the strength to say, "This is
me, flaws, scars, memories, and all. And that's okay."

As you delve deeper into these chapters and this journey of
introspection, there's hope that you not only see your reflection but embrace it fully. Everyone has a story, and
every story, no matter how fraught with suppressed emotions, is valid and valuable. Your story, with its unique blend
of joys, sorrows, triumphs, and trials, offers insights and lessons that can guide not only you but also others. By sharing
it, by standing firm in your truth, you not only liberate yourself but also potentially inspire others to embark on their
journeys of self-reflection.

There's an age-old saying: "When you become a parent, you see the world differently." It's a sentiment that rings so true for many. Suddenly, with the birth of your child, a mirror reflects not only your face but also the echoes of your past. Everything becomes clear, like a puzzle piece fitting perfectly. Your life's experiences, both the pain and the joy, the regrets and the triumphs resurface, revealing both the wounds you've healed and those you've concealed.

Isn't it funny how conversations can flow so easily, shedding light on profound truths? This is the beauty of genuine dialogue. While it seems chaotic, it brings out raw, unfiltered emotions and reflections. It's through this fluid exchange that we uncover the depth of our experiences and the significance of acknowledgment.

Now, while we're on this wave of revelation, let's dwell deeper into the concept of acknowledgment. Breaking down a life story into segments, like weeks or chapters, aids in processing. Picture it as chapters in a book or episodes in a series. Each section allows time for reflection, processing, and healing. Think of how many times you've binged a show only to realize that by the end, the details have blurred. Life is similar. We can't rush through our stories expecting clarity without taking breaks to reflect and heal. Acknowledgment is this bedrock. Once you tackle this giant, the journey becomes somewhat lighter. It's like climbing a mountain. The initial ascent is challenging, demanding every ounce of your strength. But once you've reached the plateau, you find the remaining journey smoother, the weight lighter. And here's a reality most of us grapple with: our past constantly nags, reminding us of wounds and scars. If left unchecked, these memories become towering obstacles blocking our path forward. How can one hope to navigate the future with clarity if the past remains a jumbled mess?

Our past, with its experiences and lessons, becomes our guide. It shapes us, molding our character and decisions. But for it to become a beacon, acknowledgment is essential. I've often pondered upon this very thought. What was that defining moment in my life that carved the path I'm on today? What did Vlad, the author of this book, need to confront to become the man you're reading about?

A haunting narrative from my childhood painted me as the problem. Every tear, every conflict, every challenge was supposedly my doing. The dissolution of my parents' marriage, the distance between my father and my brother, every strained relationship was attributed to my existence. This storyline, propagated by circumstances and events, cast a shadow so dark that I started believing I was the problem. Even my near-death experience as a child seemed to reinforce this belief that maybe, just maybe, my existence was a cosmic error.

But remember, acknowledgment isn't just about accepting the negative. It's also recognizing the strength and resilience that emerge from confronting these narratives. Sure, I felt like a problem, but that narrative was not the entirety of who I was. It was merely a chapter, a fleeting moment in a journey filled with potential and promise. So, as you delve deeper into this book, I invite you to join me in acknowledging our pasts, not as anchors, but as launchpads propelling us toward our true destinies.

For so long, I looked outside myself for validation. I found myself constantly seeking that nod of approval, that warm smile of acknowledgment. A recurring question that played on repeat was, "How do you move from a place of self-doubt to self-belief?" It seemed as though a void existed, and no matter how much external praise or recognition I got, it never really filled that gap. You're right. We often take on roles, narratives, and beliefs based on circumstances around us. Sometimes, we're inadvertently invited to parties we never planned – situations we never chose. As children, we have a limited understanding of the world around us. We make sense of our environment by creating stories, often without realizing the weight and permanence of these tales.

For me, the pain of feeling unwanted became a continuous narrative, and I played that role to perfection. I believed I was the problem, the outcast, the one thing that disrupted harmony. It's such a heavy burden for a child to carry, feeling like they're at fault for the brokenness around them. The realization that I wasn't the problem was revolutionary. It wasn't my choices that led to my parents' decisions or the situations around me. I wasn't responsible for their actions, their choices, their emotions. It wasn't about proving my worth to my mom or seeking validation from my absent father. And oh, the weight of that misplaced guilt – feeling like you owe someone for simply being alive. It's astonishing how therapy can change one's perspective. At first, it felt like I was speaking into a void, waiting for some divine wisdom to fall upon me. But in those moments of silence, the true healing began. My therapist allowed me to come to my own realizations, to voice my own truths, and to find my own answers.

And isn't it powerful? Realizing that the voice that matters the most is your own? It wasn't about what others told me, but about how I spoke to myself. The years of yearning for acknowledgment from others was actually a yearning for self-acknowledgment. It was a plea to see myself as valuable, not because of others but for myself. Therapy was that turning point for me. It taught me the importance of acknowledging my own worth. It made me confront my past and all its associated feelings – not as a passive observer but as an active participant. I needed to take control of my narrative.

That verse from Proverbs resonates deeply with my journey. "Hope deferred makes the heart sick." For years, my heart yearned for an acknowledgment that never came. But the moment I realized my worth, acknowledged my past, and embraced my journey, it became my "tree of life." I didn't have to wait anymore; the acknowledgment came from within. This journey of self-realization is not unique to me. Each one of us carries a story, a narrative, and sometimes burdens from the past. But if there's one thing I'd want you to take away from this, it's the power of self-acknowledgement. It's understanding that while the world may or may not give you the acknowledgment you seek, the most important validation comes from within. Embrace your story, not as a weight pulling you down, but as wings that let you soar. Your past, your experiences, your emotions – they all add up to the person you are today. Celebrate that. Embrace that. For in doing so, you unlock a world of potential and limitless possibilities.

How often have we buried parts of our past, attempting to hide away memories or experiences that evoke pain, shame, or regret? Each of us carries with us stories, incidents, or decisions that we wish had never occurred. But here's the paradox: Our attempt to bury the past often becomes the very chains that bind our progress. To truly liberate ourselves, we need to unearth and acknowledge our past, not as anchors but as catalysts for our future. Acknowledgment isn't about reliving past traumas but rather accepting them as chapters in our life's book. It's about embracing our complete narrative — both its trials and triumphs. This process, while daunting, is essential for our growth, evolution, and healing.

Take the life of Oprah Winfrey, for instance. Despite her harrowing experiences with poverty and abuse during her childhood, she didn't opt to stow them away in a corner of her memory. Instead, she channeled these adversities, drawing strength from them, and forged a path that not only led her to monumental success but also became an inspiration for millions. Oprah's perspective on failure elucidates this mindset, "I don't believe in failure. It is not a failure if you enjoyed the process." Nelson Mandela's story is another epitome of transforming adversity into an advantage. His prolonged incarceration could have been a narrative of bitterness, but instead, he spun it into a tale of resilience, hope, and a relentless fight for justice. His ethos resonates in his words, "The greatest glory in living lies not in never falling, but in rising every time we fall."

So, where does one start in this journey of acknowledgment?

**Practice Self-compassion:** Life, with its myriad experiences, often places us at a crossroads where we must confront our mistakes, insecurities, and vulnerabilities. The journey towards self-awareness starts with treating oneself with kindness and understanding. This means recognizing our imperfections and acknowledging that making mistakes is a part of the human experience. Understand that everyone, regardless of their life journey, makes mistakes. These moments are not a reflection of one's entire character but are mere chapters in a vast book. Instead of berating yourself for these slip-ups, learn from them. Every challenge we face and every error we make provides an opportunity for growth. By practicing self-compassion, you give yourself the freedom to learn and evolve, rather than stagnating in self-blame.

Be gentle with yourself. Embrace imperfections, and understand that it's human to err.

**Document Your Life Journey:** Maintaining a journal or any form of documentation is like having a mirror that reflects not just your face, but your soul. Writing offers clarity, and over time, it presents patterns, growth, and personal evolution. Chronicle significant milestones—those moments that shifted your perspective or changed the course of your life. This could be anything from graduating, facing a significant loss, to overcoming an immense challenge. Life is a blend of joyous occasions and challenging trials. By documenting both, you gain a holistic view of your journey and the resilience that has brought you through. Pen down the pivotal moments, the highs, the lows, and every lesson learned along the way.

**Celebrate Your Strengths:** While introspection often brings us face-to-face with our flaws, it's equally important to recognize and celebrate our strengths. These strengths have propelled us through life's toughest challenges and are sources of immense pride.

Every achievement, big or small, is a testament to your capabilities. Celebrate them. This doesn't necessarily mean throwing a party for every success, but it means taking a moment to appreciate your hard work and resilience. Just as there are lessons in failure, there's wisdom in success. Analyze what worked, how you approached the challenge, and how you can replicate this in future endeavors. While our missteps are part of our journey, so are our triumphs. Relish in the moments of victory and the wisdom they've imparted.

**Identify Recurring Patterns:** As you journey through introspection, you'll begin to notice recurring patterns or themes—certain habits, beliefs, or behaviors that repeatedly manifest in different areas of your life. These patterns often hold the key to deep-rooted beliefs or even past experiences that continue to influence present decisions. Whether it's a consistent approach to handling conflicts, a particular type of relationship dynamic, or even a recurring fear, spotting these themes is the first step to understanding them. Once you've identified a pattern, delve deeper. What triggers this behavior? Is there a past event linked to it? By understanding its origins, you can work towards addressing it. By spotting consistent themes in our lives, we can uncover deep-rooted beliefs or behaviors that shape our decisions.

**Seek a Support System:** The road to self-awareness, though deeply personal, doesn't have to be solitary. Surrounding oneself with a trusted support system provides both perspective and encouragement. Friends and family, who've been witnesses to your life's journey, often provide insights that might not be apparent to you. Their observations, combined with your introspection, create a fuller picture. At times, deeply entrenched beliefs or traumatic experiences might need expert intervention. Therapists and counselors are trained to guide you through these complex mazes, offering tools and strategies to cope and grow. Remember, this journey of acknowledgment is deeply personal, but you're not alone. Lean on friends, family, or professionals.

Acknowledge that this process isn't a one-time deal. It's an ongoing journey, with its own set of challenges. But the rewards — a deeper sense of self, an understanding of one's purpose, and an empowered future — are well worth the effort. To echo the empowering words of Oprah Winfrey,

"You become what you believe." Believe in your resilience, in the transformative power of acknowledgment, and in your boundless potential to craft a brighter tomorrow. Every soul carries burdens. Some of us shoulder them more heavily than others, wearing them like armor, protecting us from the piercing realities of our life's journey. As I delve deeper into these introspections, I see the universality of these experiences – the shared pain, the silent battles, and the echoes of unspoken words. My Aunt Lisa's journey embodies so much of what many of us silently endure. The feeling of perpetually living in a shadow – not one cast by any looming figure, but by the collective weight of unrealized hopes and unmet expectations. Her past experiences, including the sheer enormity of blame unfairly placed on her tiny shoulders, anchored her down, making it difficult for her to see beyond the fog of her immediate environment.

And here's a revelation – these silent burdens, these anchors that we unknowingly tether to ourselves, they can be passed on. Inadvertently, our unaddressed pain can be inherited by those closest to us, just as it was passed on to Lisa from her parents, and just as my aunt unknowingly carried the emotional baggage of her siblings. My aunt was a beacon of hope and kindness in a world that often betrayed her. A selfless soul that gave without expecting. But as I grew older, I could see past her smiles. Behind those gentle eyes, there was a sorrow – a deep yearning for something she probably couldn't even articulate herself. She was trapped in a cycle of giving and hoping, waiting for a day when the universe would finally give back.

The thing about emotional pain is that it often manifests silently. Unlike a physical wound that you can treat, emotional wounds can fester, hidden from the world but forever present in our psyche. Dementia, in my aunt's case, wasn't just a clinical diagnosis; it was a manifestation of her suppressed pain and yearning. It's essential to acknowledge the impact of these silent battles. To understand that while shortcuts might offer a temporary escape, they don't provide healing. And healing, true healing, requires introspection, acknowledgment, and action. As I sat with these reflections, a powerful realization dawned on me. The act of sharing, of verbalizing our pain, our hopes, and our journeys is, in essence, a form of healing. Through this book, and through these conversations, I'm not just sharing my journey but creating a space where others can see their own reflections. The book serves as a mirror, and in its pages, readers might find fragments of their own lives, their own unspoken pain, and their very own moments of redemption.

Lisa, my aunt, and many others have all shaped this narrative. Their stories intertwine with mine, creating a tapestry that speaks of pain, hope, and eventual healing. And the beauty of it all is that through acknowledgment, through confronting our past, our wounds, and our desires, we can pave the way for a brighter, freer future. But it all begins with a single step – the courage to acknowledge. In the quiet recesses of my aunt's eyes, I saw reflections of a universal pain — a silent plea for acknowledgment. The desperation that quietly but powerfully seeped out of her, staring out the window as if hoping for a stranger to save her from her plight, touched a chord deep within me. Her silent cries echoing, "I don't know where I am. I just feel so alone, surrounded by people who should care, but don't."

This, to me, wasn't just a personal narrative but a testament to the human spirit's resilience and its yearning for acknowledgment. We are conditioned by society to seek validation from others, often neglecting to recognize and affirm our worth. My aunt's life is a stark reminder of how one can be physically surrounded by loved ones but still feel profoundly isolated. The question then emerges: How many of us feel truly seen? Truly acknowledged?

Dementia rapidly consumed my aunt's powerful spirit. Here was a woman who had achieved so much, owning a family home, a landmark in its own right, smelling of harvard french fries, and yet, she barely lived to see it get sold. The rapid decline in her health, I believe, was not just due to old age or her illness. Instead, it was the weight of unacknowledged pain, unchecked desires, and a life of silent sacrifices that wore her down.

If only she had been given the tools, the knowledge, the words to recognize and act upon her feelings earlier in her life, perhaps she would have chosen differently. Perhaps, with acknowledgment and acceptance, she would have chosen herself, her dreams, and her desires over the constant giving and appeasing of others. What a profound lesson her life imparts — that the power of acknowledging ourselves and our desires is not a luxury but a necessity. It isn't something that should be left for the end of our lives. A confession at the deathbed or a bucket list penned in our twilight years is a stark reminder of opportunities missed and a life not fully lived. Why do we put off our dreams, desires, and needs? Out of fear? Fear of judgment? Fear of not fitting into the societal mold? This fear confines us to a life not lived to its fullest potential.

Every time I think of my aunt and the countless others like her, I'm reminded of the importance of living authentically, of seeking acknowledgment not from the world, but from within. We don't need an external reason to live — we are the reason. I am humbled and grateful to share these insights, these observations, and lessons learned. Here's to acknowledging ourselves, embracing our truth, and living life with no regrets. To live is not just to exist. It is to recognize, embrace, and celebrate our authentic selves. It's time we start living — truly living. And it all begins with acknowledgment.

# "

IN THE DEPTHS OF
ADVERSITY, WE
DISCOVER THE
STRENGTH TO SHAPE
OUR DESTINY.

**"**

# CHAPTER 2

## OF RESENTMENT, FORGIVENESS, AND MOVING FORWARD

B efore we dive headfirst into the depths of Chapter Two, let's play a little game. Let's decode some words that, quite honestly, have shaped many lives, maybe even yours. Let's break down 'resentment', 'forgiveness', and 'moving forward'. Because trust me, these words carry weight." To really grasp these concepts, let's start with resentment. Resentment is like this lingering taste in your mouth that no amount of water or gum can erase. It's birthed from unresolved feelings, turning them into bitterness, anger, and sometimes even vengeful thoughts. Why does resentment brew, you ask? It's often because those we hold dear, those who should be our safe haven, fail us. And that sense of betrayal? It leaves an indelible mark. Take a child, for instance. When they're hurt, the first thing they do is run to someone they trust, expecting solace and a fix for their pain.

But imagine if that solace never comes. Instead, they get hurt over and over. The natural outcome? Resentment.

For many, parents inadvertently become the focal point of such sentiments. There's a weight of expectations, some spoken, many unspoken. And when those expectations aren't met, resentment finds a cozy corner. "Like when I found myself resenting my mom for the roles she unknowingly thrust upon me or resenting my dad for the conflicts they both dragged me into. But, resentment doesn't just stem from direct actions; sometimes, it's the weight of generational trauma, unchecked and passed on."

*Which brings us to forgiveness. Oh, what a powerful elixir!*

Once you recognize the chokehold resentment has over you, there's a burning need for a release. Enter forgiveness. This isn't about forgetting or even justifying someone's actions. No. It's about liberating yourself from the shackles of past hurt. And as Oprah perfectly puts it, "Forgiveness is giving up the hope that anything could have turned out differently." It's an acknowledgment that while the past cannot change, your perspective can. And then, there's the act of moving forward. But what does it even look like? Is it a mere physical act, or is it more profound? Moving forward is a choice. A conscious step you take every day, refusing to let your past define your present or dictate your future. It's not about forgetting or erasing; it's about embracing, learning, and growing. This chapter is a journey through these three profound stages. The raw wounds of resentment, the healing balm of forgiveness, and the brave steps of moving forward. Each has a story, each bears lessons. And as you navigate through them, remember that you're not alone. Everyone has a narrative, sprinkled with hurt, marred by regret, but always, always, filled with the potential for healing and growth. So, are you ready to explore? To maybe see a reflection of your own journey and perhaps find a way forward? Dive in, and let's uncover these layers together.

Resentment, is like those background tabs in a browser. You keep opening them, not realizing how many are running until you find yourself overwhelmed. Just like with these background tabs, sometimes, we don't even know what's consuming our mental energy. But each background tab, every ounce of resentment, eats away at the device's performance, slowing it down, just as resentment does to our hearts and souls. Sometimes you don't even realize these background emotions are playing until they start affecting your main tasks.

I had these background emotions for 30 years! 30 years of suppressed anger towards my parents, constantly running in the background of my mind. Every memory, every conversation I had with them was tainted by these background tabs of resentment. I took a deep breath and let the weight of that realization settle in. You know, it's a lethal cycle, and these feelings keep piling up. The anger towards my dad for not wanting me. My anger towards my mother for never acknowledging my feelings. These background emotions, these 'tabs', were eating up my emotional bandwidth. But the realization? They did what they could with what they had. It's hard to accept, but once we understand that they gave what they had, the healing can begin.

Haitian culture, probably like many others, has this notion that as long as you're clothed and fed, there's no space for complaints. My mom's response every time I tried to discuss my feelings was, 'What if you were me?'" It's like they deflect, making it about them. But, deep down, they're hurting too. Their pain is so deep-seated that they can't even see past it to recognize our pain. But understanding that, it's the key to true forgiveness. Then you have the power. The power to take all those raw materials from your past and use them to build a life that you want. A life where you are in control.

I looked down for a moment, reflecting on the weight of my journey. You know, I wish more people could understand this. So many of us, especially in the Black community, are saddled with this legacy of growing up before our time. We have a lineage of children forced into adulthood prematurely. Generational trauma is real. It is, but it's time to break the cycle. This book, our conversations, it's all a step towards healing. To help people find a community, to share their stories, to lift each other up, and to understand that they're not alone in their pain.

Every story shared, every burden lightened, brings us one step closer to healing, as a community, as individuals. Our pasts, our hurts, they don't have to define us. With understanding, forgiveness, and a desire to move forward, we can reshape our narratives and build the futures we've always dreamt of.

As men normally, we'd shrug such fears off, cover them with macho bravado. Stability is a strange thing. Especially when you've been accustomed to chaos. It's almost like a tightrope walk, where suddenly the line feels too broad under your feet. For instance, when I met Julie, my first impression was, She's too nice. I told my buddies I needed someone fiery, someone unpredictable. It's what I was used to, what felt normal. But here's the thing. Sometimes, we get so wrapped up in the chaos, so accustomed to the turbulent waves, that when we're given calm waters, we can't navigate. That's a heavy realization. And it took a while to get there. I wasn't ready for Julie. I wasn't ready to be seen, truly seen, until she asked me one day, 'What's wrong with you?' Not in an accusatory way, but in genuine concern. It made me re-evaluate. It led me to therapy.

"Resentment, forgiveness, and then what?" I probed. It's about discernment. It's about recognizing patterns and understanding their origins. If you can't identify resentment or understand the depth of forgiveness, you can't truly move forward. You're onto something here.

Absolutely. Setting boundaries is crucial after forgiveness. It's the act of protecting yourself while still allowing room for connection. But it's also about recognizing how past traumas can impact present relationships. Like my friend's hesitance to commit or my initial resistance to Julie's kindness. It's all interlinked. I thought back to his analogy of background tabs on a computer. It's like those tabs again, isn't it? The unchecked ones can lead to chaos. Resentment is one such tab. But so is the desensitization to abuse. And sometimes, the chaos becomes our baseline. So moving forward, it's about changing that baseline. It's about setting new standards and expecting different outcomes.

How do we do that? By confronting the past, forgiving, and then consciously deciding what we want our future to look like. By choosing stability over chaos. By building upon the lessons learned and not just the pain experienced. I reflected on everything we'd covered. Resentment, forgiveness, moving forward – these weren't just terms.

THE EMBRACE METHOD

They were life experiences, pivotal moments that could de-
termine the course of our lives. If my story can help even
one person rechart their course, then all the pain, the struggles, the realizations – it'll all have been worth it. This
chapter felt like a spiritual and emotional catharsis, you
know? There's something transformative when you're given
the opportunity to truly reflect, unpack, and voice your experiences. It's like sifting through life's clutter and truly
seeing the golden lessons underneath. It's like diving deep
into the layers of your own soul, confronting the shadows,
and coming out with a newfound clarity. The process of
speaking, of diving into those definitions and examples, it
felt like I was healing parts of me that had been overlooked
or brushed aside for so long.

Yes, and you know what's the beauty of it? By sharing your
journey, you're paving a path for others to walk on, to realize their own struggles, to find their own healing. The
embrace method is more than just a self-help guide; it's a
beacon of hope for many. Your journey becomes a testament to the transformative power of introspection,
forgiveness, and moving forward. It's humbling, really. To
think that my journey, my experiences, can become a
source of strength and guidance for someone else. It rein-
forces the importance of the work we're doing together in
The Embrace Method.

Forgiveness is akin to removing the chains of anger, resentment, and bitterness that can hold us back. It is akin to taking off a weighty backpack that we've been carrying for years, sometimes even unknowingly. The pain and burden slowly wear on our spirits, chipping away at our joy, happiness, and our ability to truly connect with others. But the power to remove this load lies within us, through forgiveness. Reflecting on the relationship I had with my Father, I am reminded of how deep and painful wounds can run. Yet, the act of forgiving him was a declaration of taking back control over my life. I no longer wanted to be held captive by the past or allow the shadows of past hurts to dictate my future. At that Men's Conference, I realized the value of my own peace, happiness, and spiritual well-being. The act of forgiving was not about letting my Father off the hook but about freeing myself from the bondage of resentment.

My Mother's story serves as an inspirational testament to the transformative power of forgiveness. Even after enduring tremendous pain at the hands of her own mother, my Mama chose love, compassion, and understanding. By doing so, she broke a cycle of dysfunction and pain, creating a new legacy for our family, filled with love, understanding, and, most importantly, forgiveness. I am grateful every day for those invaluable moments I shared with Grandma

Josana, moments that were only possible because of my Mother's strength and capacity to forgive.

For those who are struggling with forgiveness, understand that it is indeed a journey and not a destination. Forgiveness is one of the most potent tools we possess as human beings. However, it's also one of the most challenging emotional hurdles to overcome. For those grappling with the weight of betrayal, resentment, or hurt, the path to forgiveness can seem labyrinthine and never-ending. But understand this: forgiveness is less about the endpoint and more about the journey. Each step taken towards it is a step towards self-liberation. Here are some steps to guide you through:

**Acknowledge the Pain:** Before you can forgive, you need to acknowledge and accept the hurt you've felt. Denying or suppressing your feelings will only prolong the healing process. The first step towards healing is admitting that there's a wound. Many of us, in an attempt to display strength or to swiftly move on, overlook or diminish the pain we feel. But true resilience lies in accepting your feelings, no matter how vulnerable they make you feel.

*Actionable Tip:* Start a journal. Pour your feelings onto paper. By chronicling your emotions, you can confront them head-on, making it easier to process the pain.

**Understand the Power of Forgiveness:** Recognize that forgiveness is for you, not for the person who wronged you. It's about giving yourself permission to move on and find peace. Contrary to what many believe, forgiveness isn't a sign of weakness, nor is it about letting someone off the hook. It's an act of immense strength, a gift you give to yourself. By forgiving, you're allowing yourself to break free from the chains of resentment and anger.

> *Actionable Tip:* Reflect on past instances where you've forgiven someone or someone has forgiven you. Remember the liberation and peace it brought? Use these memories as motivation to embark on your current journey of forgiveness.

**Open Up:** Talk to trusted friends or family about your feelings. Sometimes, merely vocalizing your emotions can provide clarity and perspective. Bottling up emotions is like shaking a soda can; eventually, it'll burst. Sharing your feelings with someone you trust can be cathartic. Their perspective might shine a light on angles you hadn't considered, or their mere act of listening might provide solace.

> *Actionable Tip:* Organize regular meetups with close friends or family where you discuss your feelings without judgment. These can be informal coffee dates or structured support group sessions.

**Seek Professional Help:** If your feelings are too over-whelming, consider seeking professional help. Therapists and counselors can provide guidance on how to process and overcome your emotions. Sometimes, the weight of our emotions is too hefty for us to carry alone. Therapists, counselors, and support groups offer a safe environment where you can unpack your feelings, gain insight, and learn coping mechanisms.

*Actionable Tip:* Research local therapists who specialize in grief or trauma counseling. Platforms like Psychology Today or even local community centers can be great resources. Remember, seeking help is not a sign of weakness but a testament to your commitment to healing.

**Take Your Time:** Remember, forgiveness is a journey. Do not rush the process. Give yourself the time and space you need to heal. There's no stopwatch on forgiveness. Some wounds heal quickly, while others take time. It's essential to remember that your journey is unique to you. Comparing your progress to others or forcing a timeline can hinder genuine healing.

*Actionable Tip:* Set aside a few minutes every day for self-reflection. This can be through meditation, journaling, or even a simple walk. Use this time to check in with your emotions and gauge your healing process.

Embracing forgiveness is a choice that can pave the way for peace, joy, and new beginnings. It's an act of self-love, a declaration that you won't let past hurts define your future. As you journey through life, remember to frequently reflect, reassess, and if needed, choose forgiveness. Your heart and soul will thank you. Now, it's up to you to make that choice. Reflect on those you might need to forgive and take that brave step towards healing.

# "

YOUR PAST DOESN'T
DEFINE YOU; IT
PREPARES YOU FOR
GREATNESS.

# "

# CHAPTER 3

# DISCOVERING YOUR PURPOSE: ALIGNING YOUR PAST WITH YOUR FUTURE GOALS

D o you ever feel like you're just floating through the days, weeks, and years with no real sense of purpose? It's like you're a spectator in your own life, watching things unfold without truly being involved. This feeling can be daunting, but rest assured, it's not a permanent state. By tuning into your own story and aligning your past with your future aspirations, you can ignite the path of purposeful living.

Take, for instance, Oprah Winfrey. Growing up in an environment marked by poverty and abuse, it seemed unlikely that Oprah would rise to be a global icon. But even as a child, she displayed a knack for communication. After her stint as a news anchor, she launched 'The Oprah Winfrey Show', a beacon of hope, inspiration, and personal growth for countless individuals across the globe. Through this platform, Oprah used her past as a stepping stone, not a stumbling block, propelling herself toward greatness and empowering others to do the same.

Similarly, J.K. Rowling's journey to success wasn't without its fair share of struggles. Facing challenges like being a single parent on welfare and grappling with the profound loss of her mother, Rowling found solace in weaving a tale that would go on to captivate millions. The world of Harry Potter, filled with magic, resilience, and courage, resonates with many because it is rooted in the real trials and triumphs of its creator. When you're in alignment with your purpose, the hardships or the challenges that come up, you actually see them as just that, challenges. They're not roadblocks. They're just hurdles. They're things to overcome, and you find strength and even excitement in facing them because you know that it's taking you closer to where you're meant to be. I remember a conversation I had with a friend a few years ago. He was in this high-paying corporate job and he was miserable. But the thing that struck me was he said, "It's not the tasks or the work itself that I hate. It's the fact that I feel no connection to it. I feel like it doesn't matter." He ended up leaving that job and started a nonprofit. He makes a fraction of what he used to, but he's never been happier because he found his purpose. And while the challenges he faces now are far greater than before, he wakes up every day excited to tackle them because he knows he's making a difference.

See, that's the thing. Purpose isn't just about what we're doing, but why we're doing it. That's where the real fulfillment comes from. It's not about the paycheck, the title, or the prestige. It's about alignment, feeling that you're on the path you're meant to be on. And the beauty of it all? Everyone's path is unique. Your purpose doesn't have to look like anyone else's.

I think that's something everyone reading this book should really sit with. You don't need to follow someone else's blueprint for success or happiness. Your journey, your purpose, is your own. And the sooner you can tune into that and really own it, the richer and more fulfilling your life will become.

That uneasy sense of drifting, of not really knowing where you're headed. But here's the thing: it doesn't have to be a permanent state. The past and the future are like two halves of a book, and your purpose is the spine that binds them together. Growing up, we sometimes internalize the wrong messages. But at some point, you have to step back and realize that you have a purpose. That revelation is powerful. I took a deep breath, the memories flooding back. You know, one of the most pivotal lessons I've learned is that purpose is not static, but dynamic. I first came across this idea while listening to Oprah's Super Soul Sunday. At the time, I was feeling lost, trapped in a job at Logan Airport that felt entirely misaligned with my soul. But hearing that idea—that purpose is ever-evolving—changed my perspective. I thought I'd found my purpose in the security of a steady job. But deep down, I felt a disconnect. My real purpose, the one that had been quietly tugging at my heart, was to help others. Sometimes our true purpose is hidden behind layers of expectations and external pressures. It's about helping others, about connecting with humanity, about healing and growing.

But the path to that purpose wasn't straightforward. I recall the feeling of powerlessness, the anger at my family circumstances, the aimlessness. "For a long time, my only purpose was to escape the feelings of sadness, fear, and confusion," I confessed. For me, the shift began in high school. Fitness became my lifeline, a way to regain a sense of empowerment. I started playing rugby and from there, fitness became my purpose, a way to rebuild and empower not just myself, but others.

But as time went on, that purpose began to evolve. By the time I joined the state police, I realized that my real passion was in helping people, in guiding them through their personal transformations. It wasn't about physical fitness anymore—it was about emotional and spiritual growth. Purpose isn't a static concept. It's a dynamic force that evolves and changes with us. And by aligning our past experiences with our future goals, we can create a life of fulfillment and meaning. Rediscovering purpose had changed my life, and I was eager to share that journey with others. Because when you find your true purpose, everything else falls into place.

I once lost sight of who I was at the state police. I grappled with my identity, my capability, and God's purpose for me. But through all the confusion, a profound realization struck me: purpose isn't static—it's dynamic. I had once envisioned a future for myself in the world of bodybuilding. I could see myself, standing victorious, trophy in hand. However, when I joined the state police, I felt like a shadow of my former self. Doubt crept in and eroded my self-confidence.

But then I remembered, the same discipline I had displayed in bodybuilding was still within me. When challenges seemed insurmountable, I had pushed through, honing my discipline and resolve. I had no formal training initially. Everything I knew about bodybuilding, I pieced together from forums. But I was relentless. I would hit the gym six days a week, shunning after-work drinks with colleagues, sticking to my regimen. My co-workers would ask why I was so dedicated. To them, I'd say, 'Success requires nothing less than full dedication. Half measures won't get you there.'

I faced setbacks, injuries, challenges, but I emerged victorious. I placed second and third in two categories. I wasn't necessarily the best, but I never cut corners. That's who I am. You see, when life throws you off course, you need to remember who you are. Dive deep into your core values. We all possess the raw materials we need to succeed. It might require some shaping, mentoring, or guidance, but they are there. My journey was also marked by my genuine care for others. Mentorship became a beacon for me. The police force introduced a peer mentorship program, and I jumped at the opportunity. It wasn't about money or recognition; it was about giving back. I saw a need and tried to fill it. Even when the program's standards changed, barring me from official mentorship, I found a way. I created informal networks to continue guiding young trainees."

Values guide us. When we lose sight of them, we are adrift in life's vast ocean. My father, in his own profound wisdom, would say, 'If you don't know where you're going, any road will take you there.' It is essential to align our actions with our values, for they are the compass that ensures we're on the right path. Purpose is more than just a role or a job. It's an internal compass, an alignment of passion and values. It's what drives us to be the best version of ourselves and to make a meaningful impact in the world. Remembering our past successes, understanding our core values, and staying true to our purpose are crucial steps on this journey.

It's not uncommon for individuals to feel lost, over-whelmed, or even disconnected from their own lives. The very fabric of our existence is interwoven with various experiences, memories, and choices that shape our persona. Each of us has our unique journey, fraught with challenges, triumphs, and lessons. But how can we leverage this intricate tapestry to create a roadmap for a meaningful and fulfilling future? So, where does that leave us? How do we delve into our past, pick up the fragments, and use them to build a roadmap to our future? Here's what I believe that you should do:

**Reflect on Your Journey:** All of us have stories that shape our identity. Embrace them, learn from them, and use them as your foundation. Our past is replete with stories—some uplifting, others painful, but all crucial to our personal evolution. These narratives aren't just mere events but the undercurrents that shape our identity, values, and aspirations.

*Actionable Tip:* Dedicate quiet moments regularly, perhaps through journaling or meditation, to ponder your experiences. By revisiting past moments—whether they are successes, regrets, or even mundane events—you open doors to introspection. Recognizing patterns, understanding reactions, and celebrating growth are all outcomes of this self-reflection.

**Recognize Your Strengths:** There are things you excel at, things that make your heart sing. Acknowledging these strengths is pivotal in carving out your purpose. Every individual is blessed with unique gifts. Maybe you're an incredible listener, a passionate artist, a shrewd problem-solver, or someone who can make others laugh effortlessly. It's these inherent strengths that not only make us stand out but also provide clues to our larger purpose in life.

*Actionable Tip:* Regularly solicit feedback from peers, family, or mentors about your strengths. Alternatively, self-assessment tools, like the StrengthsFinder test, can offer insights. Celebrate and cultivate these strengths, for they can guide you to avenues where you can shine the brightest.

**Understand Your Core Values:** What fuels your spirit? What are the non-negotiables in your life? Understanding your values is like setting a compass for your journey. Values are the compass of our soul. They subtly guide our actions, decisions, and reactions. Often, a sense of restlessness or dissatisfaction stems from not living in alignment with these core values.

*Actionable Tip:* Spend some time to list down what values resonate most with you—integrity, love, adventure, stability, or maybe service. Reflect on whether your current life reflects these values. If there's a disconnect, brainstorm ways to bring your daily life in closer alignment with what you deeply cherish.

**Set Tangible Goals:** Now that you have a sense of direction, what are the milestones you want to achieve? Setting clear, actionable goals will keep you motivated.

While it's essential to have a broad vision, the tangible impact is felt when these visions are broken down into achievable goals. These goals serve as stepping stones towards your larger purpose, offering clarity and motivation.

*Actionable Tip:* Practice the SMART (Specific, Measurable, Achievable, Relevant, Time-bound) technique while setting goals. For instance, instead of saying, "I want to read more," say, "I will read one book per month." Documenting these goals and reviewing them regularly can foster accountability and drive.

**Failure is a Stepping Stone:** Every setback is a lesson. Instead of seeing failures as obstacles, view them as the universe's way of teaching you something valuable. Our society often villainizes failure, painting it as an undesirable outcome. But in reality, failures are nothing but detours filled with lessons, insights, and growth opportunities. Embracing setbacks, understanding their root causes, and iterating based on these lessons can transform failures into spring-boards for success.

> **Actionable Tip:** Whenever you face a setback, instead of succumbing to disappointment, ask yourself: What can I learn from this? How can I improve? By fostering resilience and viewing failures as feedback, you can navigate challenges with grace and tenacity.

Finding your purpose is less about an end goal and more about embracing the journey. It's about continuous evolution, growth, and understanding that every chapter in your life has significance. By bridging the gap between where you've been and where you aspire to go, you pave the way for a life filled with intention and meaning.

Traditionally, we've been trained to view our life's purpose as a fixed star in the vast expanse of our universe—a singular point to which all our actions, decisions, and paths should lead. But life is not a linear journey, and neither is the discovery of purpose. It's fluid, ever-evolving, shaped by our experiences, choices, and the people we meet along the way. As we evolve, so does our understanding of what brings us joy, what ignites our passion, and where we find meaning. A purpose that feels resonant in one's twenties might shift in the thirties or forties, reflecting the different stages of personal growth and understanding.

Imagine life as a book. Each chapter, with its unique story-line, characters, and lessons, contributes to the overarching narrative. Some chapters might be about joy, others about loss. Some might teach resilience, while others introduce the concept of fleeting moments. But each one, in its unique way, adds depth to the story. Similarly, every phase of our life, be it childhood, adolescence, adulthood, or old age, presents its own set of challenges and triumphs. Instead of viewing these as isolated events, if we begin to see them as interconnected chapters that shape our journey, we start to recognize the cumulative wisdom they impart.

Every individual's journey is dotted with milestones—some visible to the world, others hidden in the heart's chambers. By reflecting on these milestones, we can decode patterns, derive lessons, and gather insights that can guide our future trajectory. The struggles faced in the past can become the bedrock of strength for future challenges. The joyous moments act as reminders of the happiness that lies ahead. By intentionally connecting the dots between our past experiences and future aspirations, we not only acknowledge the value of every experience but also infuse our path forward with a deeper sense of purpose.

You know so many times I've heard people say, 'I was just trying to get home too.' There's this constant clash of loyalties - to our partners, our jobs, the community. it's an intricate dance. Take George Floyd's death, for example. It wasn't just about one man's actions. It was about the by-standers, the other officers, torn between their duty to a superior and the obvious wrong unfolding before them. The system had chained them in a way that they couldn't act even if they wanted to. The weight of that moment was-n't just on the family. It was on those officers too, feeling powerless, voiceless against their own superior. It's heart-breaking.

There's also a broader lesson here. This internal struggle isn't unique to policing or any specific profession. It's about values. About what we stand for. It's the reason many leap into entrepreneurship. They're seeking alignment – a place where their values can shape their work. When you're stuck in a place that suppresses your identity, and your values, it's not just about losing your job or your position. It's about losing yourself. It's easy to surrender in the face of adver-sity, to let go of your identity. But the moment you do, you begin losing sight of your purpose.

Goal setting, for example, isn't just about setting bench-marks. Your purpose is your destination and your goals? They're the vehicles that drive you there. Without a con-crete plan, we find ourselves stuck in cycles, feeling like we've been in the same spot before, knowing we're not where we're meant to be but unsure of how to move. Rich Dad, Poor Dad was a game changer for me. It shifted my mindset. Made me realize that there's more to life than just working a job. There's building a legacy, finding purpose, and shaping our own destiny.

Then there's embracing failure. We often see failure as a reflection of our identity. But it's not. It's just feedback. To truly succeed, we must learn to detach ourselves from the outcome, learn from our mistakes, and use them as stepping stones. In a moment of vulnerability, I can truly say that I've had my share of failures, from career choices to personal decisions. But every misstep was a lesson, a redirection to my true calling. And when I remember that, I'm reminded of Oprah Winfrey's words, 'The biggest adventure you can ever take on is to live the life of your dreams. In the quiet that followed, one thing was clear: Discovering your purpose is a continuous journey, a process of self-reflection, alignment, and growth. It's about creating a life that resonates with who you are and what you believe in. It's about "living the life of your dreams.

Purpose is not always about grand gestures or monumental achievements. More often than not, it's found in the small moments: a heartfelt conversation, a gesture of kindness, the joy of learning something new, or the serenity of a quiet reflection. Living with intention means being present in these moments, being mindful of our actions, and understanding their ripple effects. It's about making choices that align with our values, aspirations, and the kind of impact we wish to leave on the world. When we infuse our daily life with such intention, we move away from the mechanical and step into a space of authenticity. Every action, no matter how small, starts to resonate with meaning, bringing us closer to our ever-evolving purpose. Growth and understanding are two pivotal pillars supporting the edifice of purpose. As we journey through life, we are continually presented with opportunities to expand our horizons, to step out of our comfort zones, and to redefine our boundaries.

Embracing this continuous evolution involves being open to change, being receptive to new experiences, and having the humility to accept that our understanding of life and purpose will shift with time. The dance between growth and understanding is dynamic, each influencing and enriching the other, guiding us towards a deeper realization of our purpose. And going back to what we were discussing earlier about forgiveness, I think that's where it all connects. Once you've released those burdens, those resentments, you create space for clarity. Clarity about who you are, what you want, and most importantly, why you want it. And that 'why' is where your purpose lies. It's all connected.

From forgiveness to finding purpose, it's all about inner work, introspection, and self-awareness. When you start to do the work, the pieces start to fall into place. And as we wrap up this chapter, I just want to leave our readers with this thought: Your purpose is your gift to the world. It's not about you; it's about how you can serve, and how you can make a difference. So don't shy away from it. Embrace it, chase it, and most importantly, live it. Because that's when life truly becomes magical. Until the next chapter, dear readers, keep seeking, keep growing, and keep discovering. The journey to finding your purpose is one of the most rewarding adventures you'll ever embark on.

**THE SCARS OF YOUR PAST CAN BECOME THE STARS OF YOUR FUTURE.**

# CHAPTER 4

# RELEASING NEGATIVE PATTERNS

My hope is by this point in the book, you've acknowledged your past. The weight of our past often becomes the mask we wear. It's a façade, carefully crafted, hiding the scars, the pain, and the memories that continue to haunt us. For some, this mask is adorned with laughter, joviality, and charisma. For others, it's a stoic, indifferent exterior that keeps everyone at arm's length.

I was no different. My mask was my jovial personality, a persona built on years of suppressing my emotions, years of trying to be what others expected of me. I was the class clown, the entertainer, always there with a joke or a witty comment. My laughter echoed in the halls, but my eyes, they told a different story. It's no wonder that addictions like pornography and drugs are so enticing. They offer a momentary escape, a fleeting reprieve from the burdens we carry. They are clandestine in nature, easy to hide, and provide a sense of relief, even if ephemeral. But like any mask, they too come with a price.

As I delved deeper into the memories all of my emotions flooded back. The feeling of being torn between my parents, each tugging at my heartstrings with their own narrative. The emotional manipulation. The desperate need for validation, affirmation, and most importantly, love. The realization that, as a child, I was forced to grow up too fast, taking on responsibilities and emotions that were far beyond my years.

It was during these years of turmoil and confusion that I turned to negative coping mechanisms. They became my crutch, my escape. They were my mask. When my parents separated, I became the rope in their tug-of-war. I was shown videos of my father, tears streaming down his face, claiming my mother had kidnapped me. My mother would recount stories of my father's manipulative tactics. I was caught in the middle, absorbing their emotions, their traumas, and their stories. It's painful to reflect on how I became the emotional caretaker for both my parents. How I learned to suppress my feelings, putting on a brave face, even when my heart was shattering. I learned early on that showing my true feelings was a sign of weakness. So, I buried them deep inside, often forgetting they even existed.

But as time went on, those buried feelings began to manifest in other ways. My jovial exterior was just a façade, hiding the tumultuous storm that raged within. The addictions, the negative patterns, they were all just symptoms of a deeper issue. My journey to self-awareness and healing began when I started to peel away the layers of my mask. I had to confront the traumas of my past, accept them, and find a way to move forward. I had to learn to feel my feelings honestly, without judgment or fear. It was a difficult journey, one that required introspection, self-awareness, and a lot of soul-searching. I wish I could go back and tell my younger self that he mattered. That he was loved. That he didn't need to wear a mask to be accepted. But I can't. All I can do is share my story, in the hopes that it will inspire others to confront their past, acknowledge their pain, and find a path to healing.

The mask may protect us, but it also imprisons us. It's time to set ourselves free. We all have encountered dark patterns that intertwine with our existence. These negative patterns, whether draped in the cloak of self-doubt, sewn with threads of anxiety, or patterned with the motifs of unhealthy relationships, often have their roots buried deep in our past. These patterns, if left unchecked, can tether us, preventing the unfurling of our full potential and obstructing us from living enriched lives. However, the silver lining amidst this bleakness is the undeniable truth that these patterns can be transformed. By shining the light of introspection and understanding, one can metamorphose these patterns, bridging the chasm between a turbulent past and a promising future.

The path to shedding negative patterns and embracing a life of positivity and purpose is within reach. It requires dedication, effort, and, above all, a belief in oneself. Always remember that even on the darkest nights, stars continue to shine. Similarly, even amidst challenges, your inner brilliance remains, waiting to be uncovered and shared with the world. You are not alone on this journey. Together, with knowledge as our torch and determination as our compass, we can navigate through the maze of past patterns, emerging on the other side stronger, wiser, and imbued with a sense of purpose.

The journey towards personal betterment, ridding oneself of limiting behaviors, and embracing a life rich with positivity might seem daunting, but it's entirely achievable. Let's unpack this idea further. When we talk about dedication and effort, it's essential to understand that nothing truly valuable comes easily. Just like mastering a musical instrument or training for a marathon, self-improvement requires consistent and deliberate action. These are not just vague terms; they represent the everyday choices and introspections that you commit to, understanding that every step, no matter how small, brings you closer to your desired self.

Belief in oneself might sound like a cliché, but it's the bed-rock of any personal transformation. Without a foundational belief in one's ability to change and grow, the journey becomes insurmountably difficult. Imagine a farmer who sows seeds but doesn't believe they'll grow. They might neglect to water them, protect them from pests, or provide the necessary nutrients. The seeds, in turn, don't flourish. Similarly, if we don't believe in our capacity for change, we might neglect the nurturing practices necessary for our growth.

The metaphor of the stars shining even on the darkest nights is profound. Life will undoubtedly present us with challenges, moments of doubt, or even despair. But within us, there remains an inherent brilliance: our potential, our resilience, and our unique capabilities. It's essential to re-member that these qualities, like stars, might not always be visible but are always present.

The warm embrace of July in 2001 enveloped the world outside, but within the confines of our home, a cold depar-ture was underway. My mother, summoning her inner reserves of courage and strength, decided to leave my fa-ther. As she did, a part of my world crumbled. I was engulfed in the quagmire of pain, mourning the family that once was. A storm of emotions raged within, the undercur-rents pulling me towards avenues to numb the pain.

In the absence of mature guidance and emotional tutelage, young souls like mine often find solace in maladaptive coping mechanisms. Defined as behaviors inhibiting one's ability to adjust to distressing situations, these mechanisms are usually a product of trauma, change, or illness. For me, the doorway to this perilous path was a VHS tape of the film "Basic Instinct". An unsuspecting child, I expected animated characters to dance on the screen. Instead, what unfolded was a scene with Sharon Stone, in her role as Catherine Tramell, which both horrified and captivated my juvenile self. This initial foray marked the onset of an addictive cycle.

As time progressed, so did technology. Our move to 8 Jackson Gardens came with the novel luxuries of cable television and the internet. Though the nascent days of AOL online with its iconic dial-up tone were painstakingly slow, it didn't deter my explorations. The digital realm, with its myriad of content, became an even more tempting escape. Coupled with the lack of supervision at places like the Area 4 Youth Center, the door to the world of adult content was left ajar, and my consumption grew exponentially.

The perils of pornographic addiction are manifold. Its clandestine nature, coupled with the omnipresence of high-speed internet, makes it a secret vice easily harbored. The subsequent shame, guilt, and self-loathing amplify feelings of isolation, reducing genuine human connections. Worse still, a 2018 study by Brigham Young University highlighted the neurological ramifications: prolonged exposure can diminish the brain's gray matter, impairing executive functions and potentially spiraling into depression.

My personal battle against this addiction would have continued in the shadows had it not been for a beacon of hope— my wife. After confessing my struggles to her, she, with a reservoir of empathy and grace, recommended therapy. Through years of therapeutic interventions, I confronted the ghosts of my past. My journey to recovery was less about eradicating an addiction and more about addressing the underlying trauma, negative beliefs, and familial complexities.

Yeah, managing my addiction without anyone's knowledge was my secret weapon. Well, maybe 'managing' is too optimistic a term. Hiding, rather. Laughing at it doesn't make it any less real. A vivid recollection of college flashed before my eyes, and that was of Michelle, a girl who seemed so alive yet was drowning in the vicious cycle of alcoholism. I remember my own phases, limiting my alcohol adventures to Thursdays when I resided on the campus, while the rest of the week was reserved for laundry and academics. But it wasn't just about alcohol or the temptations of pornography. It was about the reality of functioning addicts, those who had mastered the art of masking their pain, adeptly hiding behind a facade. They've made fooling themselves and everyone around them almost like a sport. I remember a time when hours would slip away as I lost myself to addiction. But the realization that there's power in vulnerability changed everything for me. We often run from the very things we should be confronting head-on.

Many of my struggles stemmed from the past – guilt for things I shouldn't have owned, projections of self-loathing, and the spiraling inability to control my behavior. Losing myself in these patterns was making me lose out on life. Addictions make us numb, keeping us stuck in a perpetual cycle of pain, and preventing us from moving forward. They steal our focus and direction. If you don't know who you are, you give others the power to define you. Just because my family lived in certain conditions doesn't mean I have to. Their journey is a motivator for me to chart a different course.

Let me share a brief anecdote to emphasize this point:

Janet, a close friend of a friend, went through a challenging divorce. She was left with two young kids, a mountain of debt, and a heart full of pain. For months, she described her life as being trapped in an endless, stormy night. She felt her spark had vanished. But with time, support, and introspection, Janet started to rediscover herself. She began attending therapy, joined a support group, and embarked on a journey of self-care and reflection. One night, as she sat in her garden, looking up, she told her son, "Even though the clouds of my life seemed endless, tonight I can see the stars. And just like them, I realized my spark never left. It was just momentarily obscured." Today, Janet runs support groups for women going through similar challenges, helping them find their stars amidst their storms.

To continue from the metaphor, the sentiment "you are not alone on this journey" holds immeasurable weight. Humanity's shared experiences mean that even in isolation, others have faced similar battles, felt the same pain, and most importantly, found ways to overcome. There's a collective wisdom available to us, a treasure trove of insights and lessons that can guide us through our personal mazes.

To have knowledge as our torch means to be armed with information, awareness, and understanding as we navigate through life. Knowledge illuminates our path, ensuring we don't stumble in ignorance. Determination, on the other hand, is our unwavering commitment to the journey, regardless of how treacherous the path becomes. With these two tools, the maze of past patterns, which represents our entrenched habits and behaviors, becomes navigable. It's no longer a confusing entanglement but a challenge we're equipped to tackle.

The path to transcending our limiting patterns is akin to a journey through a dark forest. But with our inherent brilliance, the shared experiences of others, and equipped with the torch of knowledge and the compass of determination, we're not just wandering aimlessly; we're on a purposeful trek towards a brighter clearing. Remember, the journey itself fosters growth. Each step, each challenge, and each victory, no matter how small, shapes us, preparing us for the joy of emerging into the light stronger, wiser, and with a renewed sense of purpose.

Every individual possesses the innate power to transcend these boundaries. Let's delve deeper into the process of personal liberation from these shackles. Every journey starts with a step, and the first step towards transforming negative patterns is recognizing them. This is an inward journey, an exploration of the inner realms of our mind. It involves being brutally honest with oneself. What are the repetitive thoughts, feelings, and behaviors that seem to pull you down? These are the anchors, the chains, that hold back the ship of your potential. By illuminating them, you take the first stride towards breaking free.

Just like a plant, every negative pattern has roots. It didn't just appear; it grew from something. This stage requires a descent into one's past, a revisitation of memories, events, or learned beliefs that contributed to the formation of these patterns. Often, understanding where a pattern originated can be pivotal in addressing and dismantling it. This phase might be uncomfortable but is essential for genuine transformation. Now, armed with understanding, it's time for a direct confrontation. This phase is about questioning these negative patterns. Why do they exist? Are the beliefs that support them accurate? For example, if you constantly feel you're 'not good enough', is that a fact or just a belief? Such rational analysis can unveil that many of our negative patterns are built on shaky foundations. By challenging them, we start the process of breaking them down.

Imagine clearing weeds from a garden. If you don't plant flowers in their place, the weeds might just grow back. Similarly, as you work on breaking negative patterns, it's imperative to replace them with positive habits. Techniques such as mindfulness and meditation are not just spiritual tools but are also scientifically backed methods to improve mental clarity, emotional health, and even physical well-being. Embracing these practices offers a double advantage: they suppress the negative while nurturing the positive. Humans, by nature, are social beings. Our interactions play a significant role in shaping us. As you tread this challenging path of transformation, having a supportive environment is invaluable. This could be in the form of trusted friends, family members, or support groups. They serve as sounding boards, cheerleaders, and occasionally, mirrors reflecting our progress or lack thereof.

Tools like Covenant Eyes go a step further, providing not just support but also constant vigilance, which can be particularly useful when addressing addictions or deeply entrenched habits. For far too long, society has viewed vulnerability as a weakness. But as visionaries like MyRon Edmonds have showcased, vulnerability is an asset, a window to authenticity. By accepting and expressing our vulnerabilities, we not only heal ourselves but also offer others the courage to do the same. It's in these raw, genuine moments that true healing and connection occur. He created a community called "The Men's Winning Circle." A community and safe space where men's vulnerability is not only encouraged but celebrated. He taught me that our greatest superpower lies in our ability to be vulnerable with ourselves and with others. We will discuss vulnerability and seeking support in more depth later on in this book.

# "

RESILIENCE IS THE ART OF TURNING SETBACKS INTO COMEBACKS.

"

# CHAPTER 5

# BUILDING RESILIENCE: OVERCOMING ADVERSITY AND THRIVING DESPITE STRUGGLES

L ife is full of challenges, and we all face adversity at some point in our lives. But what sets truly successful people apart is their ability to "mine their own gold." That is, grow through and learn from struggles and use what they've learned to enhance theirs and others' lives. This ability is known as resilience, and it's a critical necessity for achieving success and happiness.

Joining the ranks of the Massachusetts State Police was, at the time, one of the most challenging undertakings of my life. I had taken the Civil Service exam in 2013, while in college, scored a 98.6 and 99 on the State and Municipal exams respectively, and heard nothing until over three years later. At the time, I was working as Teen Program Director in my hometown of Cambridge, and ultimately decided to participate in the rigorous the selection process, which included a mile-and-a-half timed run, obstacle course, psychological exam, and a thorough background investigation. Though each of those events had their challenges, they nowhere near prepared me for what I would experience at the actual academy.

The State Police is a paramilitary organization, meaning they observe many if not all military courtesies, ranking structures, and standard operating procedures that are synonymous with armed forces. As such, the Massachusetts State Police holds a reputation of being one of the most challenging police academies in the country, and my experience affirmed that. Every minute of the sixteen-hour training day is accounted for. Every meal, class, activity, personal item, issued gear, and shortcoming involving the same are documented and supervised. My initial nickname, (which are as plentiful as they are hilarious in the academy) was Louisiana, probably because it was close enough to Louissaint and didn't require the use of additional brain cells. Little did the drill instructors know that my name would be one they would not forget.

Less than two months in, I had returned home for the weekend on a Friday evening after another grueling training week, when my maternal Grandmother Josana Jean-Charles, who had been living with us for nearly 17 years, passed away after a long battle with illness Gran Josana's health took a sharp decline back in 2009 after learning that one of her daughters passed away. As my Mom was still working full-time, the weight of meeting her growing list of needs fell on my brother Serge and I for the next eight years. Between her dementia, multiple infections, and life-saving amputation a year before her passing, caring for my Grandmother was, as they say, the longest goodbye I will have ever said to a loved one. As painful as her passing was, I chose to tell no one at the academy. I returned the following Monday morning to a cumulative exam that I barely studied for, and prepared mentally to bury Grandma the following weekend.

A mere two weeks later, on a sunny Friday the 13th, first platoon and I were falling out (that means departing) of morning formation after chow and heading to our first class of the day, when I felt a sharp and gas-like pain in my lower abdomen as I was double-timing to Alpha building. I thought to myself, "man, those breakfast sausages are giving me the bubble guts!" However as I settled into my classroom seat, the pain quickly transformed from mild and uncomfortable to excruciating. WARNING: this story is not for the squeamish. My platoonmate saw me writhing in pain and sweaitn profusely next to him, and suggested I went to the bathroom before the instructor arrived to square myself away. I obliged. I later landed in the medical unit, escorted by my Drill Instructor and that same classmate, which after a quick examination found me being rushed to the local hospital, where I discovered I suffered a testicular torsion (an unpreventable condition in which the a testicle rotates and twists the spermatic cord, which carries blood to the testicle. I was told that the twisting (or torsion) had blocked the flow of blood to the testicle and caused swelling, pain, and if left untreated would lead to tissue death. One emergency surgery, second emergency visit, and four days later, I was already back at the State Police Academy.

Although I could not run and PT with my classmates, I pushed through the pain of my injury and continued on with my studies. My enthusiasm would be tested once more as I was recovering, when I failed the third cumulative written exam of our training. I was eventually sat down by a panel of high-ranking Troopers of the MSP Academy, who were concerned that I would not have enough grade points, between missing several weeks of physical training and failing my third exam, to graduate from the State Police Academy. One Trooper even went as far to suggest that I medically defer to the next class. In this moment, I I had not idea how I woulc heal myself faster-what I DID know for sure, was that I would either return to the academy as a Trooper or never again. I put everything on the line for this opportunity. I paid off my car, bought all of the materials, and resigned from my position instead of taking a leave of absence. I HAD to succeed. I can't tell you exactly what changed by making that decision, but doing so made it possible to heal and get back to physical training, retake and pass that exam, and graduate from the State Police Academy, not even at the bottom of my class.

Life, in its unpredictable nature, brings about both peaks of joy and valleys of challenges. The sentiment that struggles are not intended to shatter us, but rather to construct us, presents a refreshing perspective on adversity. It urges us to perceive challenges not as dead-ends but as stepping stones leading towards growth and self-realization.

Every challenge we face, be it personal, professional, or emotional, brings with it a spectrum of emotions — despair, frustration, and even hopelessness. Such feelings, while natural, can become overwhelming, causing individuals to lose sight of their purpose and passion. But think about it; when did a profound transformation occur in the absence of some resistance? Much like the butterfly struggles to emerge from its cocoon, only to spread its wings in all its glory, we too, are molded by our challenges.

To elucidate this point, consider the process of refining gold. Raw gold ore is subjected to intense heat. This daunting process, as punishing as it seems, purifies the gold, eliminating impurities, and enhancing its value and brilliance. Similarly, our struggles, as heated and demanding as they can be, have the potential to refine us, revealing a version of ourselves that's purer, stronger, and infinitely more resilient.

The key, then, is not to escape challenges but to engage with them constructively. One might ask, "How does one hold onto hope when weighed down by the gravity of struggles?" The answer lies in remembering our 'why'. Before embarking on any journey or endeavor, we are fueled by a sense of purpose, a clear vision of our destination, or the change we wish to bring about. This original motivation is our anchor. Amidst storms of doubt and waves of setbacks, revisiting this 'why' can offer solace and direction.

Now, let's dive deeper into the tangible strategies one can adopt to nurture resilience:

1. **Practice Gratitude**: The power of gratitude lies in its simplicity. By acknowledging and appreciating the good in our lives, we train our minds to focus on abundance rather than lack. This isn't about ignoring challenges but choosing to see the full picture. For instance, maintaining a gratitude journal, where you note down three things you're grateful for each day, can gradually shift your perspective, making you more resilient in the face of challenges.

2. **Reframe Negative Experiences**: Every cloud has a silver lining, they say. The art of reframing requires one to view challenges not as setbacks but as setups

for a comeback. For instance, losing a job might be seen as an opportunity to pivot careers, acquire a new skill, or even take that entrepreneurial leap.

3. **Develop a Support System**: Humans, by nature, are social beings. In our moments of doubt, having someone to lean on can make a world of difference. Whether it's the encouraging words of a spouse, the wise counsel of a mentor, or the empathetic ear of a friend, a strong support system acts as a buffer against life's blows. For example, during grueling training at the state police academy, surrounded by new challenges and rigorous demands, having a circle of loved ones to share, vent, or seek advice can significantly bolster one's resilience.

4. **Take Care of Yourself**: The mind and body are intrinsically linked. Physical well-being can significantly impact mental resilience. Regular exercise, a balanced diet, adequate sleep, and activities that elevate mood are not luxuries but essentials. Think of it this way: you wouldn't expect a car to run efficiently without regular maintenance. Similarly, our bodies and minds require consistent care to navigate challenges effectively.

5. **Set Goals and Take Action**: The act of setting goals, no matter how small, instills a sense of purpose.

Moreover, taking consistent steps towards these goals, even if they are baby steps, can foster a feeling of achievement and control. This proactive approach acts as a counter to feelings of helplessness that challenges might bring about.

While struggles are an inherent part of the human experience, they do not define us. Instead, how we respond to them does. By cultivating gratitude, reframing experiences, leaning on support, prioritizing self-care, and adopting a goal-oriented approach, we can navigate the choppy waters of adversity, emerging not just unscathed but fortified. As the Japanese proverb goes, "Fall seven times, stand up eight." Your journey of resilience is not marked by the absence of falls but by the tenacity to rise, learn, and march forward every single time.

Remember that building resilience is a process, and it's okay to take things one step at a time. By practicing gratitude, reframing negative experiences, developing a support system, taking care of yourself, and setting goals and taking action, you can overcome past struggles and thrive in all areas of your life.

Building resilience is a crucial skill for overcoming adversity and thriving despite past struggles. By cultivating a mindset of gratitude, reframing negative experiences, developing a support system, prioritizing self-care, and setting goals and taking action, you can build resilience and achieve success and happiness in all areas of your life. Just remember the words of Nick Vujicic: "Life isn't about having limbs, it's about having courage.

# "

DON'T LET YOUR
WOUNDS BE YOUR
SHACKLES; LET THEM
BE YOUR WINGS.

# "

# CHAPTER 6

## CULTIVATING GRATITUDE: FINDING JOY AND APPRECIATION IN EVERY EXPERIENCE

G ratitude is a transformative emotion that has the capacity to change our lives. It helps us focus on the beauty of each moment and celebrate the good, no matter how trivial. The very act of recognizing and acknowledging these moments instills a positive mindset, paving the way for happiness, resilience, and success.

In my journey, gratitude has been a beacon, shedding light even in the most challenging situations. It's taught me to find goodness in relationships and situations that were once a source of pain. To forgive is to understand that events and people cannot change what has already transpired. In forgiving my father, in forgiving my mother, I realized the essence of gratitude. At this juncture of writing my story and launching my program, one might wonder, what does gratitude mean to Vlad now?

Well, I've always been fond of metaphors. So, let me paint a picture. Before embracing gratitude, I visualized life's challenges as a balloon filling up with air, ready to burst any moment. Every setback, trauma, or abandonment felt like added pressure, making me fear that I was about to explode. This perspective had me constantly on edge, unable to handle any adversity. But now, that very balloon has taken on a different form. It doesn't fill upwards, dangerously close to popping; it expands outward. This change in perspective means that despite the challenges or hardships I face, there is room to grow, adapt, and stretch without the fear of breaking. Even in my most trying times, like my tumultuous relationship with my mother, I've learned to see an opportunity for personal growth and to help others.

Gratitude is an emotion that possesses transformative power. By cultivating gratitude, I focus on the myriad of blessings in my life, no matter how insignificant they might seem. This perspective shifts the mind from dwelling on what's missing to celebrating what's present. This mindset not only enhances our happiness and resilience but also sets us on a path to achieving greater success.

One might think it's straightforward to be thankful for the apparent joys in life. However, true gratitude goes beyond that. It's about finding the silver lining even in challenging situations, difficult relationships, or with those who might have wronged us. One pivotal understanding that has helped me navigate these complex feelings is realizing that forgiveness is accepting the past without wishing for a different outcome. It's releasing ourselves from the bonds of resentment and allowing healing to commence.

Reflecting on my past, I remember the times I forgave my father and mother. The act of forgiving was more for my peace than theirs. It helped me redefine what gratitude means to me, especially as I embarked on this new journey of writing and creating a program that might change lives.

For a better understanding, consider this metaphor: Before I truly embraced gratitude, I envisioned life's challenges and setbacks as an ever-inflating balloon. With each adversity, the balloon filled more and more until I felt I was on the brink of bursting. Today, with gratitude as my guide, I imagine myself as that same balloon. But instead of just inflating upwards, I'm expanding outwards in every direction. This expansion isn't just about personal growth; it's also about sharing that growth with others.

God has given me the capacity to rise above challenges, teaching me that life's adversities aren't happening to me but for me. This shift in perspective allows me to see challenges as opportunities to grow and then share that growth with others in need. Whether it's supporting my cousin Steve or a friend facing family struggles, I now have the capacity to offer help. And it all stems from gratitude.

By being truly grateful, I'm anchored in the present, appreciating all that I have. Whether it's the tenants in my house, my loving family, or even the old car that serves its purpose – there's so much to be thankful for. This mindset allows me to escape the vicious cycle of always wanting more out of envy or resentment. Instead, I want more for the right reasons.

Les Brown once said that many live "lives of quiet desperation." I've been there, feeling trapped in a job I despised. Yet, by learning to be grateful, even for that very job, my outlook began to shift. I realized that rather than resenting the present, I could strategically utilize my current position to achieve my future aspirations. Even through physical pain and adversity, I've learned to seek the lessons they offer.

In essence, gratitude has given me freedom. It has liberated me from desperation, allowing me to live authentically. For anyone embarking on a journey of self-discovery, understanding and embracing gratitude is vital. It provides clarity, purpose, and above all, a joy that permeates every experience.

Gratitude, for me, is like a shield against negativity. It's a voice that reminds me that challenges aren't there to break me but to mold me. The adversities I once rued, I now see as a chance to expand my horizons and extend my wisdom to others. Is there a secret to this transformative mindset? It's simple – gratitude. It releases the shackles of negativity, whispering a gentle reminder that life's trials aren't punishments; they're opportunities for growth. This sentiment changed my perspective from "Why is this happening to me?" to "How can I use this to benefit someone else?"

For those seeking the essence of a grateful heart, consider this: gratitude is the very lifeblood of joy. It's the foundation on which contentment is built. It eliminates the desperation many feel in their daily lives, replacing it with hope and purpose. As Les Brown wisely put it, "Many people live lives of quiet desperation." But with gratitude, that desperation dissipates, replaced by a sense of purpose and direction. So, as I reflect upon my past, where I once cursed my job or lamented about life's challenges, I now find gratitude in each moment. Every obstacle becomes an opportunity, every challenge a lesson, and every moment an occasion for thanksgiving. Gratitude, in essence, is the key to unlocking life's greatest treasures. It's the pathway to true contentment and unbridled joy.

Gratitude, as I've come to understand it, is more than just an emotion; it's a way of seeing, of being. It's in those moments when you're knee-deep in adversity, yet you look up and see the silver lining of the cloud above you. It's in the remembrance of love, even after forgiveness. And for me, the journey to cultivating gratitude was as winding as the Charles River itself. There's something to be said about being grateful in situations that challenge us. I once bore a heavy heart of resentment, particularly towards my parents. Yet, it wasn't until I walked the path of forgiveness that I could recall, with fondness, the moments that once seemed lost in the whirlwind of emotions. Every river has a source, a beginning that shapes its journey and determines its flow. My river, the Charles, started with my father. He was the force that, knowingly or unknowingly, set many things in motion in my life. The Charles River in Cambridge wasn't just a body of water for me; it was a testament to the fluidity of life, memories, and the role of gratitude in shaping our perceptions.

My father was an enigma. On the surface, he presented the facade of a content man, but hidden deep within were the scars of his past. His early life was not an easy one. Growing up without a father and bearing the burden of poverty, he experienced trials that left lasting marks. These weren't just scars; they were open wounds, which affected not only him but all of us. Our family felt the aftershocks of his trauma.

It's a tale that many can resonate with - the experiences of one generation invariably spilling over into the next.

But to understand a river, one must trace it back to its source. My father's pain was rooted in his experiences. His father had children with another woman and passed away before legitimizing his relationship with my grandmother. This scenario left my father and his siblings to grapple with not just the stigmatization but also the very real challenges of growing up in a third-world country without a guiding hand. Every person he met, every decision he made, was colored by these early experiences.

Yet amidst these challenges, were the moments of joy. Those Sunday afternoons when we walked alongside the Charles River were pockets of happiness. We started our ritual with a casual stroll to the Star Market. It was our time - he with his newspaper and I with my wrestling and video game magazines. From there, our journey took us past MIT, weaving our way to Harvard Square. Despite the length of these walks, they always felt too short, leaving me yearning for more.

It's curious how moments from our past can shape our present and dictate our future. I realized this profoundly during that October morning in 2020. While my job at Logan International Airport wasn't my dream, it was there that another force, Trooper Larry, redirected my course. Larry was more than a colleague; he was a beacon of hope. His persistent badgering, always highlighting the power of my voice, ignited a spark. It was his belief in me, his constant reminders, that made me believe in my own potential.

But life, as it often does, threw a curveball. Amidst a routine inspection, the sudden discharge of my pistol momentarily plunged my world into darkness. It wasn't just a physical jolt but an existential one. Questions swirled in my head. Why did this happen? Was it a sign? And, as I soon realized upon my return to work, it was indeed a cosmic nudge, pushing me towards my true calling.

At times, our paths are marred with obstacles, making us question our direction. After the incident, my superiors' response wasn't one of concern but blame. It's easy to harbor resentment in such circumstances. But, drawing from my father's experiences and our walks by the Charles, I sought a deeper meaning. I found solace in the belief that there was a higher power guiding me. The incident wasn't a setback; it was a message, reminding me of my true purpose. The path forward was clear. I immersed myself in the world of voice acting, learning, growing, and expanding my horizons. Every critique, every lesson became a stepping stone, pushing me towards my dream. And as I reflected on my journey, gratitude became my compass. It reminded me to appreciate not just the highs but also the lows, understanding that each played a pivotal role in shaping my destiny.

Yet gratitude, like any virtue, isn't innate; it requires nurturing. Here's how I cultivated it:

1. **Embrace Memories**: Delve into your past, embrace memories, both good and bad. Each has shaped you, made you who you are today.

2. **Engage in Reflection**: Regular introspection, whether through journaling or quiet contemplation, allows us to recognize and appreciate the myriad blessings in our lives.

3. **Act**: Giving back, whether through volunteering or mentoring, allows us to see beyond ourselves, recognizing the larger tapestry of life and our role in it.

4. **Affirm**: Positive self-talk is powerful. Celebrate your achievements, and remember your worth.

5. **Express**: Don't hold back your gratitude. Express it, share it, spread it.

Gratitude, like the Charles River, flows, enriches, and nourishes. It has the power to transform perceptions, heal wounds, and illuminate paths. As I journey forward, it's the memories of my father, our walks, the challenges, and the victories that remind me to be ever grateful, to see beauty in every twist and turn.

Cultivating gratitude is a powerful tool for unlocking many a great gem from our life's experiences  By keeping a gratitude journal, practicing mindfulness, giving back, practicing positive self-talk, and expressing gratitude to others, we can transform our mindset and create a more positive, fulfilling life. We deserve to take some time to appreciate the blessings in our lives and cultivate a mindset of gratitude that can lead to greater happiness and success. As Oprah Winfrey once said, "Be thankful for what you have; you'll end up having more. If you concentrate on what you don't have, you will never, ever have enough.

**IN THE DARKEST MOMENTS, WE FIND THE BRIGHTEST OPPORTUNITIES FOR GROWTH.**

# CHAPTER 7

# SELF LOVE: THE EMBRACE
# YOU NEED THE MOST

B y this point in your journey through this book, you have
done a lot of important and inspiring work together. You've shed light on your past traumas, learned
how to release negative patterns, discovered ways in which
you can build resilience, and community and learned how
to extinguish hopelessness through harnessing the unique
power of gratitude. All of these practices are essential to
living a fulfilling and authentic life, and once I started practicing them myself, I was lead to the most difficult journey
for me to sustain in: self-love.

In a world where comparison and self-doubt often reign su-
preme, it's crucial to cultivate a deep well of self-love and
self-acceptance. These qualities serve as the foundation for
personal growth, happiness, and a life lived authentically.
Embracing who you are and cherishing your unique journey is not only liberating but also empowering. This chapter

is dedicated to helping you embark on a transformative journey of self-discovery, fostering a profound love for yourself, and accepting the magnificent person you truly are.

I did not learn what it meant to truly love and accept myself until I was in my thirties. This is because it would take years for me to embrace, process, and reframe negative feelings about myself that were born in childhood. My Mother and Father's relationship was rife with arguing and separation,and I couldn't help but wonder why. I grew up watching families like the Cosby's, Bankses and Winslows navigate tough conversations and resolve their issues as a family. It always brought me jot to see everyone come together at the end of the episode despite having hurt each other in the process. Even *Sister Sister* had two families living under the same roof and they still managed to get along with each other; so, why couldn't we? So one day, after plenty of witnessed fights, I decided to ask my Mother. "Mom, why do you and Papi fight all of the time?" My Mother answered: "Well, it all started to get worse when you were conceived son. Your Father did not want you, and hounded me to get you aborted throughout my entire pregnancy. Since then, we've been like this." I realize today that my Mother did the best she could in the moment to answer my question, but she and I had no idea how profoundly that information would impact me and my self-esteem moving forward. The notion of my own Father not wanting me both confused and disturbed me, especially because he gave me the most positive attention out of everyone in the house. He would take me to arcades on the weekends, buy me Friendly's Sundaes, and even get me the videogames I wanted. Why would a person do these things if they didn't want that person around? What was more, was that I sat on this information for years without ever confronting my Father about it, and in kind, he never brought it up.

When my parents separated when I was ten, my already fragile self-worth took another blow. In having conversations about this time period later in life, my Mother recalled a particular statement I made to her shortly after we moved into our new apartment. I told her, "Well, if all of these problems between you Dad, and Serge got worse after I was born, maybe I shouldn't have been born at all." My poor Mother not having all of the tools to protect me emotionally and also having to be strong for her two sons-did her best to assure me that she chose me, because God did. "He wanted you to live," she said, and "your life is a miracle." I wanted to believe her, but as time went on, I began to increasingly resent myself for existing. Although most in my family saw me as a happy child worthy of attention in praise, in my mind, I was to blame for my parent's terrible relationship. My existence allowed my Father to mistreat my brother and act like he didn't exist. I, was inherently problematic. Without healing, forgiveness, or gratitude, these pervasive thoughts silently grow in strength.

They give way to self-medicating and addiction, sabotaging relationships and opportunities to be loved and celebrated, and if left untreated for too long, can even result in self-harm, or suicide. As I mentioned earlier, I as many of us do, have a tendency to face the music only if it is blaring in my face and obliterating eardrums in the process. Body-building, dancing, and being the funny guy did little to solve how very little I thought of myself, which of course was firmly linked with the anger I had towards my Father. The greatest wake-up call-to-action to love myself came unsuspectingly, one cloudy weekday morning in February. On this day, I felt the full weight of the negativity I had been allowing to fester into my mind. My morning routine at that time usually consisted of a 4:00am rising and gym session, followed by a nice shower and time to meditate before leaving for work at 7:00am. None of those things happened this day. I sluggishly rolled out of bed and instantly felt exhausted. The dread I usually had about going to a job I grew to hate felt greater than ever. What was supposed to be a 7:00am departure from my home became 7:45. I didn't care if I were late.

I didn't care about anything. That morning, it was as if there was a voice in my head persistently telling me:

"Nothing you do matters, and there's no point in trying." A good friend of mine reached out to me that morning and was having a tough time following a loss in her family, and I internalized every bit of her grief. I questioned why God would allow good people to suffer so much. Where I would normally be strong, I felt weak and defeated. As the day went on, the negative thoughts continued on loop-and for each minute that passed I felt less hopeful than the last. Sunken deeper than I've ever been, I quickly found myself overwhelmed and overrun with despair, and would later find myself in a private bathroom stall in my office building, on my knees, with my job-issued .45 caliber pistol held close to my head-and in a split moment of desperation-pondered whether or not pulling the trigger would finally bring me the relief I needed from being such a failure.

I quickly got to my feet and said, "Man I'm trippin'" holstered my weapon, and finished out my day rather unremarkably before going home. I did what I always did and buried that memory in busywork and distractions until Friday of that week. I had just arrived home from work and was backing my cruiser into its respective garage bay. I stepped out briefly to retrieve the mail from our mailbox. Not ironically, I was talking to my other best friend from college-the husband of the friend I spoke to earlier that week- and we were checking in about our weeks. He mentioned he was well in spite of having "fought his demons," and it was then I realized what happened Tuesday, and said to myself, "my God, I really could have killed myself." I was suddenly overcome with grief, shame, and shock. The reality I hid from was now literally crashing into me, and despite crying alone in my cruiser for what seemed like forever, I was still inclined to put on my best "I'm doing okay" mask as to shield my wife from my 'mess.' As I walked up the stairs to our ground-level apartment in the duplex we owned, I did my best to stuff the tears back in the ducts from which they were pouring endlessly from, and entered our bedroom, where my wife was watching TV. "I can do this," I thought, "just hold it together long enough and change the subject as soon as you can."

All Jul asked me was how my day was, and I crumbled. I confessed my heart to her, told her all about Tuesday tearfully-and hysterically in pockets-and how scared, tired, and ashamed I was at the thought of devastating her and our families. Jul, aligned in her spirit of care, nurture and grace, held me close, allowed the tears to flow, and reaffirmed me that she would love me no matter what, as we both navigated this storm. Throughout the years, I would often ask myself what I did to ever deserve such a strong, loving and faithful woman-but on this day, I was just grateful to have her.

Sometimes in life, when our unchecked emotional wounds fester into crisis, we create even more massive burdens for ourselves in trying to *contain* what is meant to be *shared* with others who love and care for us; *especially* as men. Although I experienced several breakthroughs in talk therapy for the past 7 years, self-doubt, low self-esteem and hopelessness were still elusive foes I had yet to best. Here I was, at rock bottom, depressed, emotionally destitute and completely depleted, and YET, stubbornly committed to being okay. I was not. And what I learned as I navigated healing from this revelation, was that loving myself was NOT optional; it was as necessary as it was unfamiliar-and most importantly, I learned that I could not win this battle in the same way I have been trying to-**alone**. It was time to ask for help-the failure of which was literally a life or death situation. I made it my priority to reframe the way I saw myself. I had to deconstruct the lies I *told* myself *about* myself. I had to unlearn the destructive way in which I starved myself from love by focusing on public achievements. As it turns out, that vulnerability would reveal to me perhaps the best tool I never knew I needed to combat my self-hatred: **community**, which we will discuss further in the next chapter.

Okay. So we've talked about why it's important to love ourselves, but *how* can we tangibly experience it? Here are some steps to get you started:

1. **Accept what is true, release what is not:** Many of us internalize traumatic events that happened early in life, and in time convince ourselves that we we did something to deserve the negative treatment. Loving ourselves requires that we reframe those experiences in truth and grace within ourselves. When reflecting on such an event or hurtful treatment another gave you, say aloud to yourself: "It it was out of my control then, but I am in control now." You now have the opportunity to teach yourself, and others how to love and treat you.

2. **Embracing Imperfection:** Perfection is an illusion that often leaves us feeling inadequate. Instead of striving for an unattainable ideal, embrace your imperfections as beautiful expressions of your humanity. Recognize that mistakes and setbacks are essential components of growth and learning. Embrace your flaws as stepping stones to self-improvement. When you acknowledge and accept your imperfections, you liberate yourself from the weight of unrealistic expectations and open the door to self-acceptance.

3. **Shedding the Masks:** Throughout life, we often wear masks to conform to societal expectations or to hide our true selves. It's time to release those masks and allow your authentic self to shine. Embrace

your quirks, passions, and idiosyncrasies. Unveil the unique aspects of your personality that make you who you are. By honoring your true self, you not only attract genuine connections but also inspire others to do the same.

4. **Cultivating Self-Compassion:** Self-compassion is the tender embrace of your own humanity. Treat yourself with the same compassion, understanding, and forgiveness you would offer a dear friend. Acknowledge that you are human, prone to making mistakes, and deserving of love even when you stumble. Practice self-compassion by reframing self-critical thoughts into messages of self-kindness. Replace "I'm not good enough" with "I have enough, I do enough I *am* enough."

5. **Be True to yourself:** Embrace your desires, dreams, and values without apology. Tune into your inner voice and trust your intuition. When you live in alignment with your true self, you radiate a magnetic energy that draws in opportunities, relationships, and experiences that resonate with your soul.

When I think of self-love, I had to clarify that self-love hasn't really been until later in life. It is something that I'm still teaching myself and I'm still experiencing. But when I have experienced it, and as I experience it, I experience a great deal of gratitude for myself, for the gifts God has given me. The person that I am today, and the essence of who I am always. And that's something I'm still teaching myself to do, even when there are challenges laid in front of me that would test my self-esteem. Self-love is letting go of the lies that I hold myself which kept me from appreciating me. It's loving and accepting. it's also important to understand in my journey the opposite of self-love with self-hatred and loathing. And I wouldn't have known what self-love's was until I took these steps of embracing gratitude, forgiveness, healing, and building community. I realized, I've been spending a lot of my life not liking myself, telling myself lies to debase me and to keep me from realizing my full potential. I was almost scared to love myself because if I did, I felt like I was losing something on the other end. I was either losing the favor from my parents, or feeling guilty about the destruction around me. So when you grow up in a dysfunctional, chaotic home with, with abuse and neglect, you develop a survivor skill set.

One day, my cousin said to me that I've always exuded confidence. I really had to figure out what that really meant. Let's break it down. My ego kept people at bay. So they couldn't see how unconfident I was deeply inside. In order to really be confident you have to accept who you truly are. Not the boy who wasn't wanted within the womb. Not the child that was in the middle of a conflict. Not the person who was described as being the nail in the coffin of his parents' marriage, or the reason why his brother was mistreated the way that he was.

Those were all conditions that I did not create, I only realized who I truly was when I asked God to see me through his eyes as he created me. I would actually assert more that these are all qualities that I had all along. You just never truly accept everything that you've been equipped with in this world. Each of us has an influence that we need to unleash on the world. So we cannot afford to get bogged down with self-hatred, loathing, regret, and anger. When we're not in a place of healing, we are actively hurting ourselves by replaying those messages. We lose so much time And so much of your life on negativity.

For a long time, when I first met my wife, I was afraid for her to meet my family. I always kept people an arm's length. I didn't want anybody to love me because I associated love with hurt and abandonment. So here comes my wife, who is more than I could ever imagine and I froze. Previously I had only chosen to love people who couldn't love me back. I could not love myself. so I naturally had a type. My type was people who couldn't love me.

If we haven't taught ourselves and given ourselves love, we don't have the capacity for it, right? So, she was the antithesis. Because in order to receive love, you have to be vulnerable enough. She said you are not who you think you are. You're not who you tell yourself you are. You are worthy of love, and you are worthy to receive love.

She didn't run away from you because she could see the hurt in me, but saw the person beyond that. When we met, she was in grad school finishing up her last year in her Masters of Social Work program. She was equipped with the tools. Nobody ever really cared before her and I believe that everyone just needs somebody to lean on.

I think back to my bodybuilding show in 2016, I just wanted to do that because I was competitive and I wasn't about to lose. I didn't take loss well. I had to believe that I was capable to a degree. And self-love is not something you can buy or a plan that you can follow. It's something that is intrinsic within, and everything else in your life builds upon it. It wasn't until I had the suicidal ideations that I really was confronted with feelings of being emotionally bankrupt. It is my goal to assist you in not feeling that way.You have children, you advance in your career, and you genuinely embrace yourself with all your strengths and flaws? The possibilities are limitless.

Just like with credit, it's not about having a negative past or mistakes that we've made. It's about understanding, reconciling, and then using the new knowledge and growth to propel ourselves further than we ever imagined. When we recognize our worth and truly love ourselves, it opens doors to opportunities and experiences we previously thought were impossible.

Loving oneself is like giving yourself a new credit score. Every step you take towards self-appreciation, acceptance, and love improves that score, allowing you to leverage greater things in life.

you have children, you advance in your career, and you genuinely embrace yourself with all your strengths and flaws? The possibilities are limitless. Just like with credit, it's not about having a negative past or mistakes that we've made. It's about understanding, reconciling, and then using the new knowledge and growth to propel ourselves further than we ever imagined. When we recognize our worth and truly love ourselves, it opens doors to opportunities and experiences we previously thought were impossible.

Loving oneself is like giving yourself a new credit score. Every step you take towards self-appreciation, acceptance, and love improves that score, allowing you to leverage greater things in life.

And sometimes it takes someone else, like my wife in my case, to hold up a mirror and make you confront the reality. For me, the realization was, if I was able to achieve this much when I didn't love myself, then the sky's the limit now that I do.

So to anyone reading this, understand that self-love isn't just about feeling good. It's about unlocking potential, achieving dreams, and genuinely living a life that's fulfilling. Because at the end of the day, if we don't love and believe in ourselves, then all our accomplishments, no matter how grand, will feel empty.

It's about having a full heart to accompany a full life, and realizing that the journey of self-love can be both challenging and rewarding. But once you embark on it, there's no looking back – only forward to a brighter, more loving future.

Self-love is not a destination but a lifelong journey. It starts with nurturing, kind and embracing relationship with yourself. Take time each day to appreciate the qualities that make you unique. Reflect on your achievements, no matter how small, and celebrate your progress. Remember: we are greater than the hurtful things that have been said or done to us. Self-love is seeing ourselves through the lens through which God fearfully and wonderfully made us: as beautiful, sought-after, and loved beings in his image. Embrace your passions and indulge in activities that bring you joy. Treat yourself with the same kindness and care you would extend to a loved one. And when those tough days come, recall these inspiring words of the late-great Maya Angelou:

> *"You alone are enough. You have nothing to prove to anybody."*

# THE PAIN YOU'VE ENDURED CAN BE THE FUEL THAT PROPELS YOU TO YOUR DREAMS.

# CHAPTER 8

# CONNECTING WITH OTHERS: HEALING YOUR WOUNDS THROUGH CONNECTING WITH COMMUNITY

Perhaps the most dangerous lie we can fall prey to, is the one that tells us we can handle all life to throw at us alone. As humans are social creatures, and our connections with others can play a critical role in our emotional well-being. When we feel isolated or disconnected, it can be difficult to heal from traumas and move forward in a positive direction. However, by cultivating meaningful connections with others, we can find a sense of belonging and support that can help us heal and thrive.

A rule of thought that plagues mine and many conservative Caribbean families is that whatever occurs within the family, should remain, and only be discussed within the family. which *realllly* means, seldom to never at all. In other words, telling your teacher or best friend about the belting you received last night, is a NO-GO. Talking through the experience of living with cockroaches and mice is forbidden, and sharing family stories of any kind is treasonous. The reason behind the secrecy? Well, it was twofold. First, sharing personal stories could give another person the ammunition they need to hurt you in the deepest ways possible but throwing your personal woes in your face. Second, the only person anyone needs to talk to about their problems, is Jesus Christ himself; confession to Him and Him alone resolves all issues. I took this convoluted rule as gospel, and naturally, stuffed nearly all of my painful life events and feelings into myself and kept them from being weaponized against me. What I've learned, and I mean the hard way, is that staunch vows of secrecy always create more issues for us, whether we are withholding trauma that creates inner-turmoil, or avoiding vulnerability and sharing altogether with the people we love, which proves difficult at having and enjoying meaningful relationships. The truth is, our lives are meant to be **SHARED**. And while every opportunity to share your spirit may not be appropriate, the practice alone allows us to connect to much needed resources and supports that can help us heal and prosper.

I had to literally learn how to ask for help at the lowest point, after I considered giving up and taking my life. I recall a conversation I had the following week with my friend, mentor and sponsor, Preston, that I widely consider a turn-ing point in the way I approached self-care. Having met in a social group dedicated to helping aspiring speakers mon-etize their stories, what started as a message to Preston about his EPK blossomed into a crucial friendship that I didn't know I was missing in my life.

Preston is an awesome soul, and what is truly unique about our relationship is that I can rely on him to tell me what I **need** to hear, when I likely **don't** want to hear it, in a way that is both **direct** and detailed. Having one or several people like this at your disposal allows one to have account-ability, and practice the habit of receiving tough and fair feedback for growth.

Painfully as I walked the bustling downtown Lowell neigh-borhood, I told Preston what happened the Tuesday prior and he replied something to the effect of, "THIS IS NOT A GAME. YOU NEED TO CHECK IN WITH ME, AND CONNECT WITH AT LEAST FIVE PEOPLE EACH DAY-YOU NEED TO BE IN MEETINGS EVERYDAY-I'M SERIOUS MAN, DON'T F%#& AROUND WITH THIS," he said firmly in his Southern twang. I could tell that when I shared my story with Preston, he didn't mince words because he cared about me and knew that without the proper community support in place-especially in my fragile state-I would be in dangerous territory. I took what

Preston told me that day with all of the seriousness that he intended. It was from there that I began aggressively building out a robust support system, that allowed not only for weekly release of my emotions but for daily release.

I first contacted my therapist Martin, whom I had been working with for seven years at that point, and bumped our bimonthly meetings back up to weekly sessions. Given the seriousness of recent events, Martin was more than accommodating for my new schedule.

Preston had also told me about a support group called ACA: Adult Children of Alcoholics and Dysfunctional families. This is a 12-step program that closely follows the traditions of Alcoholics Anonymous, but what was special about it for me, was that it provided so much literature about the dysfunctional family dynamics that can exist with or without substance use. It was as if the founders of this support group crafted their language and traditions from right inside my childhood home. Every morning at 7:00am via teleconference, I learned about the "laundry list-" 14 traits of an adult child-a term I would grow comfortable using to describe myself-and accepting, or *embracing* the traits that applied to me proved extremely useful in understanding how I got to rock bottom.

One trait in particular, number 10, was particularly relatable:

> *10. We have "stuffed" our feelings from our traumatic childhoods and have lost the ability to feel or express our feelings because it hurts so much (Denial)*
>
> *Tony A., 1978*

What's more, is that there was another list, called the "flip side" of the laundry list, that when recited each day helped me shift my mindset from that of a victim, to that of a victor. That is, coming out of denial, accepting what was, and empowering myself by stating what *is* and will *be*.

> *The flipside of #10 is as follows:*
>
> *10. We come out of denial about our traumatic childhoods and regain the ability to feel and express our emotions.*

When I felt up to it, of course, there were always opportunities for those wanting to share their responses to the daily reading, or anything else for that matter, to do so in a friendly safe space. After a few listens I jumped right in, and "came out of denial" about my childhood experiences, "broke the no-talk rule" as ACA says, and to always be thanks and reminded at the end of my share that I was "heard" was the validation and listening ear that I was missing. Although there was often upwards of twenty-some-odd strangers on the line each morning, I eventually knew that I was among friends.

In addition to individual therapy, daily ACA calls and check-ins with Preston, the real game changer in my community team was becoming a member of The Men's Winning Circle- a men's support group dedicated to helping "men win in the things that matter." My good friend and mentor Frantz, who also happened to be my realtor and my cousin Steve's best friend, told me about joining this group in the later months of 2021, and this seemed like the most appropriate time to check it out. In fact, by way of small group coaching the organization offered each week, MWC was the first group of people I opened up to about my suicidal thoughts. The subsequently continuous love, affirmation, accountability and prayer I received from my small cohort made me feel like it was all going to be alright- and that I was capable of living a life I could be proud of. The magic in the MWC for me was in how vulnerability-an experience often outlawed among black men-was both encouraged and touted as our superpower. I am still a member of this important and diverse conglomerate of mostly black men today, and through it I have made several friends that have become business partners, mentors, and prayer partners.

I traveled to Maryland only a few months after my rock-bottom to attend the very first MWC conference, and what happened there would radically change my life. The theme of the conference was the "Father Wound," and MyRon Edmonds along with several filled the two-day conference with various opportunities for networking, reflecting and of course, prayer-but it was the final day that shifted me permanently. MyRon spoke often of his own Father wound, and how it impacted him as a man, Husband and Father; but the surprise came in when MyRon introduced his Father to the stage, who tearfully and powerfully shared his own traumatic childhood story of abuse and dysfunction. At the end, they would join each other on stage, sharing their story of reconciliation while a large graphic of a father and son pair of silhouettes displayed in the background. The picture depicted the father, missing many pieces of himself, handing a nearly complete son the final piece of him that he needed to be whole.

Their story was a powerful tale of pain, abuse, anger, sadness, generational trauma, healing, and forgiveness. Before I knew it, every man at that conference was at the base of that stage, ready and eager to receive prayer from the Father-Son minister duo, but also, to release the hurt feelings we all harbored towards our Fathers.

There are few experiences in life that are out of body-and this was certainly one of them. The Holy Spirit flowed through that crowd unlike anything I've ever witnessed. Dozens upon dozens of grown men-some as young as me, and others old enough to my Father-crying, praying, some even yelping as they finally experienced the grief of Fatherlessness that was hidden behind anger for many years. We prayed together and over one another, cried together, embraced each other with hugs, and let it all go. At the end, the final call to action was for each of us to return to our seats, pick up our phones, and text our Fathers. In that text, we were challenged to acknowledge our Fathers as having done the best they could with what they knew, apologize for any of our wrongdoings, and finally, to let them know that we forgave them, and we loved them. Many of us lingered in our seats with those instructions, some of us even crying harder than we were moments before.

In that time of hesitation, the pride that protected the teenage Vlad from my Father's cruel words as I moved out of his home for the second time my junior year at CRLS-sprung its head to protect me once again. All of the painful childhood memories, including the day I confronted my Father about not wanting me-came flooding back, tempting me to disassociate from the anointing that was this experience and be stubborn. But by the Grace of God, I opened up my messages and sent a tearful message to my Father, telling him that I knew he did the best he could, thanked him for all he has done for me and taught me, that I forgave him. My Father, who often takes hours to text back, re-sponded swiftly, thanking me for his forgiveness, and even confessed that he "never felt that he belonged," yet was thankful for having me in his life.

I cannot understate the momentous impact this conference had on my personal development. From the moment I sent that text to my Father, I instantly felt lighter-my soul felt free, and although my Father would have his moments here and there down the road, I could no longer be angry with him. It was truly a miracle I long held was impossible to experience, and all it took, was me willing to ask for help. Today, in the course of life's ups and downs, I know exactly where, when, how, and **_WHO_** to ask for a helping hand.

So how can we connect with others and find healing from life's harshest battles? Here are some tips to get started:

1.  **Join a local support group:** You can also look for online support groups that focus on topics related to your past experiences, such as trauma, addiction, or grief. Like the MWC or ACA, connecting with oth-ers who have gone through similar struggles can be a powerful source of healing and support. These groups are a great way to practice sharing your story and learning from other people share theirs in a safe space. I always recommend support groups to those

who are not yet ready to participate in traditional therapy.

2. **Establish a Robust and Diverse Support System:** As one of my mentors always tells me, there is never such a thing as too much help. The more safeguards you have in place (i.e individual therapy, journaling, support groups, accountability partners, etc) the easier you will bounce back when you slip up or have setbacks.

3. **Attend events and social gatherings:** Look for local events, such as community festivals or workshops, and attend them with an open mind. This can be a great way to meet new people and expand your social circle.

4. **Reach out to friends and family:** If you feel disconnected from your loved ones, take the initiative to reach out and connect with them, even if you think they don't want to. Make plans to spend time together and share your experiences and feelings.

5. **Practice empathy:** When connecting with others, try to put yourself in their shoes and see the world from their perspective. This can help build understanding and compassion, and deepen your connections with others. What's more, is that the

more you can practice active listening while others share, the more you can learn from their story.

Remember that connecting with others is a process that takes time and effort. It can be difficult to open up and share our vulnerabilities with others, but the rewards can be immense, and even life-changing. If you feel intimidated by support group settings, identifying even just one person you can trust with your feelings is a start. .

Having a community is a powerful necessity in living a happy life, for healing from our past and moving forward in a positive direction with like-minded people. By joining support groups, attending events, reaching out to loved ones, and practicing empathy, we can cultivate meaningful connections that can help us find a sense of belonging and support. I encourage you to take a moment to reach out to someone today, and connect with the community around you. Afterall, never know how someone or a group of people you meet, may change your life forever.

Whenever I find myself reflecting on the concept of community, an overwhelming sense of gratitude and clarity envelops me. To me, community is not just a word or an abstract notion. It's a life-saving, essential force. Community is a diverse system of support comprised of individuals who love you, challenge you, and accept you without reservations. It's their collective presence that gives one strength and resilience.

The significance of community became clear to me during one of the darkest episodes of my life. Had it not been for the community I'd formed around myself, I might not be here to tell my story. Their support was the lifeline I didn't know I needed, particularly when I was grappling with the thought of ending it all.

My journey with community began rather unexpectedly. That one day where I humbled myself and spoke to Preston. Our exchange turned into an hour-long conversation, the beginning of a deep bond. It was this relationship that illustrated the power of community for me.

Preston became more than just a mentor; he became my sponsor. When I was drowning in my darkest thoughts, he was the voice of reason that pulled me back from the abyss. His insistence that I embed myself in community, that I never let isolation become my refuge again, was both a challenge and a promise. He underscored the importance of connection, of being part of something bigger than oneself.

During my formative years, isolation was a coping mechanism. Emotional isolation became my shield against the volatility of my parents' arguments. The echoes of their confrontations were so intense that solitude became a safe haven. But it was a double-edged sword; while it protected me, it also kept me away from seeking help.

Had I understood the significance of community earlier in life, perhaps my journey would have been different. Maybe I would've leaned on my brother more, sought solace with my cousins, or even opened up about the chaos at home. Because community isn't just about sharing the good times; it's about holding each other up during the storms.

The importance of participation within a community is paramount. You might have numerous support systems around you - a church, a school, a club - but unless you actively participate and engage, their potential remains untapped.

Today, I want readers to understand the transformative power of community. It can start small – maybe just with a notebook or journal where you pour your heart out. But eventually, it can blossom into a network of relationships that sustains and uplifts you. To me, one of the most profound realizations was the idea that community is the ledge that helps you climb out of rock bottom. No matter how deep the abyss, with the right support, you can always find your way back to the light.

# ABOUT THE AUTHOR

Vladimir Louissaint is a charismatic soul who was proudly raised in the vibrant city of Cambridge, MA. Vladimir was born with a magnetic presence and an unwavering passion for life, which has brought him down many roads, from Personal Training and youth work, to Law Enforcement and acting. The greatest experience of his life thus far, however, has been as a Husband and Father.

For bookings and appearances please contact:

**Vladimir F. Louissaint**
Owner, *Voices By Vlad, LLC*

 (857) 251-3755
 *voicesbyvlad@gmail.com*
 *voicesbyvlad.com*
 *40 Essex Street, Lowell, MA Apt. #1 01850*

Don't forget to follow him on social media:

Instagram – @vladlouissiant
Tiktok: @vladthebullspeaks

Made in the USA
Middletown, DE
06 November 2023